The Obscure and Fun Facts of the Faroe Islands

A Travel Guide and Alternative Introduction to Faroese Society and Culture

Rúni í Múla

ISBN: 9798227855930

Self-published by author

First published in 2023

Contents

Preface

This book is made as an effort for a new and more interesting take on a traditional travel guidebook, with many interesting stories, facts and places worth visiting. To me, visitors always seem to see and visit the same places and are mostly presented with the same stories. With this book, I have tried my best to provide you with all that isn't presented normally so that you might have the best experience while visiting the Faroe Islands. This has been my motivation for making this book.

The book is structured in two main parts. One is about fun and fascinating facts about the Faroes. At the same time, the second is a unique travel guide, where many places are highlighted that aren't usually accessible to tourists, but also inducing some of the most visited places worth visiting. Also, in this section, I have highlighted some of the best things to do during your stay and a list of important phone numbers and contact information, including some safety guidelines that will help you during your stay.

If you read the book out of pure interest, the book's first part is for you. If you plan on travelling to the Faroes, the first part can serve as a cultural introduction, while the second will serve as the travel guide that will give you the best experience you can have while staying. However, know that if you decide to discuss some of this book's contents with locals, chances are that they haven't heard about many of the fascinating facts and stories in these pages.

Wishing you a pleasant reading and a great stay in the Faroe Islands, should you decide to go.

Rúni í Múla

May 2023, Kunoy

Introduction

North of Scotland, between Iceland and Norway, in the rushing North Atlantic Ocean, there is a small isolated archipelago with high mountains and harsh nature. These are the Faroe Islands - one of the world's smallest nations.

The archipelago comprises 18 small islands distinguished by steep cliffs, tall mountains, narrow fjords, and a population of some 50,000 people.

The Faroese language is descended from Old Norse, the language spoken by the Norsemen who settled the islands 1200 years ago.

The Faroese have defied harsh nature and living conditions for centuries. Today, it is a nation with one of the highest living standards in the world. A highly industrial economy based primarily on fisheries and aquaculture thrives, while a Nordic welfare model ensures everyone can realise their full potential. The Faroe Islands are well-known for their maritime expertise and export seafood to all six continents.

The Faroe Islands are strategically located between Europe and North America and are only a few hours' flight from major cities in Northern Europe. The scenery upon arrival provides visitors with a captivating natural experience in a society with advanced infrastructure and digital networks.

Centuries of relative isolation have preserved ancient traditions that shape life in the Faroe Islands to this day. Faroese society is distinguished by its unique blend of traditional and modern culture, which fosters a strong sense of local community and an active outlook as a globalised Nordic nation.

With this book, you will get an alternative introduction to the Faroese society with all the strange, interesting and obscure facts and fascinating insights about life on the islands, which you won't find in any other history- or guidebook. Additionally, this book contains recommendations for all the must-sees and does if you decide to visit the islands.

I hope you'll enjoy reading it and that this book might serve as a conversation starter should you decide to visit the Faroe Islands.

Chapter One

Denmark, not Denmark

The Political Satus of the Faroe Islands

In the Færeyinga saga, the Story of the Faroe Islanders, it is said that the first Viking settlers were Norwegian emigrants who, because of high taxes, sought to Iceland. On their way, they came to the Faroe Islands, and some of the Norwegians decided to stay there. The Færeyinga saga tells of the famous folk hero, Sigmundur Brestisson, who brought Christianity to the islands around the year 1.000 and did so in the service of the Norwegian king, Harald Hairfair. Since then, the Faroe Islands became part of the Kingdom of Norway and stayed under Norwegian rule until 1814. Norway entered the Kalmar Union in 1397, and during that union, Norway eventually came under Danish control and remained in the Kingdom of Denmark until the Treaty of Kiel in 1814. When Norway gained sovereignty, the Faroe Islands, Iceland and Greenland continued within the Danish kingdom.

Today, the Faroe Islands have become a self-ruling territory, which might be hard to understand from an outsider's perspective because if it's not a sovereign state and not a Danish County, then what is it? This often becomes evident in geopolitics when the Faroe Islands try to become part of international associations because the state definitions seldom fit the reality of the Denmark/Faroe relationship.

The Danish and Faroese flags. Graphics by Rúni í Múla

The Danish Constitution

The Constitutional Act of the Kingdom of Denmark (Danmarks Riges Grundlov) is the Constitution of the Danish Kingdom of Realm and is one of the world's oldest constitutions. It was first adopted in 1849 and has since been replaced with newer revisions. The latest revised version is from 1953, explicitly mentioning the Faroe Islands and Greenland in several articles.

Faroese politicians have often discussed whether the Faroe Islands ever adopted the Constitution and whether the Faroe Islands should recognise the Constitution. These politicians are typically on the nationalist political wing, while most non-nationalists recognise it. But politicians across all the political spectres have also asked whether the Constitution represents the actual relationship between Denmark and the Faroe Islands, many of whom argue that the Constitution in several areas has been outdated from the political practices and agreements that exist between the two nations. Some have also argued that the Home Rule Act is against the Constitution. Nonetheless, the Constitution is the binding legislation granting the Faroese self-rule via the Home Rule Act.

Independence or Home Rule?

During the Second World War, the Faroe Islands were under British administration, and during those years, the ties to Denmark were completely cut off. When the war settled and Denmark was free from German occupation, the future of the relationship between Denmark and the Faroe Islands was uncertain. Denmark proposed a Home Rule Act like Iceland before they voted for independence. Still, the Faroese parliament wouldn't recognise this new Danish law, even though it meant the Faroe Islands would gain self-governance. Therefore, an independence referendum was decided, and the citizens could choose between two options. The choices were:

1. To adopt the Home Rule Act

2. To get independence from Denmark

Two political parties were against the vote because they wanted more options. Therefore, the People's Party asked their supporters to write "no" beside option one and to vote for option two, while the Social Democrats advised their voters to do the same thing, only the opposite. The referendum participation was 67,5 %, of which 4,1 % of the votes were deemed invalid. The result was 50,7 % for independence and 49,3 % for home rule. In that way, the referendum's result was a slight yes for independence. Still, because the results were so close and because of the low participation rate, the Danish officials did not recognise the result, stating that such decisions with such fundamental changes should have a more apparent result.

So, the independence vote was not recognised, and instead, the Faroe Islands got its Home Rule Act, giving the islands extended self-governance. This law contained two lists, List A and List B, where particular political areas were highlighted that the Faroe Islands could gain complete control without political discussions with the Danish authorities (List A) and areas that could be overtaken through political negotiations (List B).

By 2005, most of the listed areas had been overtaken, and therefore, the Home Rule was extended by two additional laws which expanded the Faroese autonomy regarding fisheries and international affairs.

Chapter Two

Operation Valentine

The British Occupation During World War II

From the 12th of April 1940 to the 10th of June 1942, the British Military occupied the Faroe Islands under an operation called *Operation Valentine*. This was just after the German invasion of Denmark and Norway on the 9th of April 1940, which occurred only three days before. On the day before the German invasion, Winston Churchill said that the British army had discussed the North Atlantic situation and decided to occupy the Faroe Islands. On the 12th of April, two officers came on land in Tórshavn and announced their arrival. The day after, 250 soldiers arrived in a foreign country, many of them believed to be Norway.

The British occupation proved to play a crucial role in the development of the Faroese society. It was the British military that made the first airport, and they also built roads in many places where no roads had been before. They brought the cinema with them and taught the Faroese people modern dance, which is still called *Eingilskur dansur*, English dance. Sweets and chocolate were also first introduced, and to this day, you can still buy

English brands such as Dairymilk and Digestive biscuits, even though most of the imported goods on the Faroe Islands come from Denmark.

During the occupation, the Faroese society saw a transformation which had never been seen before. At times, as many as 8.000 British soldiers were on the islands and during their stay, many Faroese / British marriages took place, and many children were born.

Soldiers by a canon in Nes, Eysturoy. Photo by Leutnant Taylor, the Imperial War Museums.

Faroe or Pharaoh?

When the war started and men were sent to the Faroe Islands, some soldiers ended up in Egypt. Because of the name Faroe, British military officials thought they meant Egypt, mistaking the Faroes for the Pharaohs.

A young graduate who had just finished his studies in Middle Eastern Studies was interviewed for a position in the British Intelligence Forces. At the interview, he was asked what his credentials were. He told them he spoke and wrote Arabic and could also read hieroglyphics. The interviewer then asked him what hieroglyphics were, and he replied that they were the written language of the pharaohs. The young scholar was, therefore, sent to the Faroe Islands.

Fights Over Women

During the occupation, the British soldiers were very well integrated into Faroese society. They lived amongst the locals throughout the country, and many British-Faroese marriages occurred during this time. Many children were born, which explains the many different English last names still found today.

Compared to the average Faroese man, the British soldiers were well-dressed in their uniforms. They could dance and play instruments and were said to be very well-mannered. They did not share the same drinking habits as the Faroese, many of whom were binge drinkers.

This made the Englishmen much more desirable to many of the young women of the time than the average Faroese man. The Faroese men also noticed this, often leading to a fight or two, especially during the weekend dances.

Often, when dances were held in the local theatre in Tórshavn, the British soldiers would only allow Faroese women to come inside. In contrast, the men weren't allowed to enter but had to wait outside, and had they been angry with the soldiers beforehand, this didn't make the situation any better. Especially outside this theatre, many quarrels were between the men from Tórshavn and the British soldiers, and similar stories have also been told in Vágar.

Faroeitis

Soldiers who had fought in close combat in battles in Europe and who had escaped without any physical harm were sometimes stationed in the Faroe Islands during the occupation. These were traumatised soldiers who had experienced high stress on the battlefields of the European mainland who were now in a place where no battles were fought and where there seemingly was no danger other than the air strikes and the mines floating in the sea around the archipelago.

While the British soldiers stationed on the island of Vágar had to be hard-working as they were building a primary military base, constructing roads, and even building an airfield situated where the modern airport is today, many of the soldiers stationed at other locations on the islands had close to nothing to do and were caught in severe boredom.

Then, a British military doctor noticed the condition he would later call *Faroeitis*.

The signs of Faroeitis started with the soldiers becoming depressed because of the high stress they had had in their battles in Europe, combined with the boredom they were experiencing now that they had no daily routines and were free of any danger. The second stage of the condition was the soldiers reporting that the sheep had started speaking with them. In this condition's third and final stage, the soldiers began talking back to the sheep.

Faroeitis, some then concluded, was the psychological condition caused by spending too much time in the Faroe Islands.

Graves and Roses

The soldiers who died during the British occupation were buried in the cemeteries around the islands. In many of these cemeteries, memorial statues are raised to remember the soldiers who died during the war. Like in British military tradition, English roses were planted in front of the gravestones so that when the sun rose and set throughout the day, the shadow of the roses would, at some point in the day, lie on the graves of the fallen soldiers.

Merkið - Recognition of the Faroese Flag

Initially drawn in 1917 by Faroese students studying in Copenhagen, Denmark, the Faroese flag Merkið was first known as the student flag. Even though the students insisted this be the official Faroese flag and that many Faroese people took it to them and used it on their boats and their flagpoles, the Danish authorities never recognised the flag.

Since the Faroe Islands and Denmark were occupied by the two enemies, Great Britain and Germany, it became a dangerous affair for the Faroese fishing vessels to sail under the Danish flag. Because of this inconvenience for the Faroese fishing vessels and because of safety measures, Merkið gained its formal recognition on the 25th of March 1940 by the British military, making it possible to differentiate between Danish and Faroese fishing vessels and ships.

English Food and Candy

Even though many years have passed since World War II ended, the influence of the British troops can still be seen today. The roads the British built are still very much in use but have, of course, been updated, and the airport is still located at the same site that the British chose during the occupation.

Those who were children during the war have told many stories about the English soldiers. Many mentioned English candy and chocolate, which the soldiers sometimes gave to the children. Back then, chocolate and even fruit were rare on the islands, and therefore, the children were all very excited when they got these goods from the soldiers.

Even though most of the imported goods to the Faroe Islands come via Denmark, a considerable proportion of biscuits, tea, candy, and chocolate are still imported from the United Kingdom. This is why many English brands otherwise unknown to the rest of Europe can be found in every Faroese supermarket.

Military training in Skálafjørður. Photo by Leutnant Taylor, the Imperial War Museums.

Chapter Three

The Death Penalty

Is That Still Legal?

Historically, death penalties have been a part of the Faroese jurisdictional system and go back to Viking times. Though such penalties are believed to have been common, which the Færeyinga saga, the Viking traditions in general and some Faroese placenames indicate, nothing is recorded before the late 1500s.

In the 1600s, however, many recordings revealed that the penalties they used at that time were severe. People were often sentenced to long imprisonments, sometimes in holding cells with total darkness. The prisons have been located in several different places throughout Tórshavn, in Skansin (the old fort), Myrkastova (a basement in Tinganes) and other areas in Tinganes that today serve as parliament buildings. The sentences are believed to have been harsh, but people were usually let go when they reached their breaking point. Many men have been sentenced for work, sometimes for a specific period, other times for life. But, like in most other countries, people were sometimes also sentenced to death, and the harshest punishments recorded are death by hanging, drowning and beheading.

The first recorded death sentence was for a man from the island of Svínoy who was found guilty of incest. Though he is mentioned in "Jarðarbókin" from 1584, 1588 and 1590, nothing is known about his case. The assumption is, however, that he was executed in the local "Thing" in the northern islands. The oldest documented case was in 1615, when a man was sentenced for impregnating his wife's sister. They were both sentenced to death, and even though the means of their demise weren't mentioned, the man was expected to be beheaded, and the woman drowned.

Stealing was a severe crime, and the sentence for stealing sheep was death by hanging. Many such corrections have been made for repetitive theft. According to the law, witchcraft was forbidden and sentenced to death by burning, but even though the law was in action, and some were accused of witchcraft, no one was ever found guilty.

The last time someone was sentenced to death was in 1706 when two half-siblings from Streymoy conceived a child. They were both beheaded in Tórshavn.

Many of the sentences have been for incest, but the legal definition for incest, according to the law, was the relation in seven generations. This law was hard to uphold because the population at that time was low, which made it hard to follow this rule and still expand the population.

Often, when young women were sentenced to death, the Faroese officials tried to postpone their judgment, which they did by appealing to the Danish king. The far distance between the Faroes and Denmark meant that it took a long time to get a proper sentence in place, and when the king finally received the message and had decided on their fate, many had already fled the islands with foreign merchant ships.

Though the death penalty was the harshest sentence, many torture methods were used. It was common to see people flagged in public, where they would be stripped bare and whipped up to 39 times. Afterwards, the one whipped had to pull a chain with two large, heavy stones from the town centre and all the way to the outfields. This was to ensure that he or she would remember his or her misdeeds and so that they wouldn't commit the same crime they had done before.

Other scare tactics were also used. When someone was decapitated, the heads and sometimes other limbs were often attached to a pole outside the old fort to scare others into committing the same crime.

The executioner was paid handsomely. He was paid regularly and had a stable salary, and in addition, he would get paid extra whenever he had to execute a sentence, mild or harsh. But society back then was small. Unlike in other countries, where the executioners could disguise their identity by wearing a mask, the executioner couldn't keep his identity a secret in the small town of Tórshavn. Therefore, it was difficult to get anyone to apply for the job, and sometimes, when someone was sentenced to death, there wasn't anyone to execute the sentence. Therefore, he was sentenced to work as an executioner.

Seyðabrævið (1298). Book of Lund, Unknown Author.

The Sheep Letter

It is a widespread belief in the Faroe Islands that Seyðabrævið, the Sheep Letter, contains the death penalty for stealing sheep and that this law technically was in action until 2004, when the Sheep Letter was finally revoked. This is not true.

Seyðabrævið is dated the 28th of June 1298 and is the oldest document written on the Faroe Islands. Unlike the Færeyinga saga, which was written in Iceland only a few years prior, Seyðabrævið is written in Kirkjubø by the famous bishop Erlendur, who is known by some of the old legends. Erlendur was bishop in Kirkjubø and had the Kirkjubømúrurin built, which caused great outrage between the northern and the southern parts of the Faroes. He demanded high taxes from the people, which started a civil war. According to the legend, he was killed during the war, but historical documents suggest that he fled to Norway around that time.

Seyðabrævið is a legal document from the early Middle Ages. It exists in two original versions. One is kept in the National Archive in the Faroes, while the other is kept in a museum in Lund, Sweden, bound in a book with other historical Swedish documents from that time.

Contrary to popular belief, the letter does not contain a clause authorising a death sentence. The idea hereof, however, might stem from mixing up the old practices of sentencing sheep theft with the letter regulating different sheep matters.

The Military Act of 1937

The old Danish Military Act of 1937 concerned all parts of the Kingdom, including the Faroe Islands and Greenland. When Denmark got a new law in 1973, the law did not concern the Faroe Islands; therefore, the 1937 law was still in action. § 37 in the Military Act from 1937 says as follows:

No life sentence may be carried out before the King[1] has decided not to exercise his right of pardon. The court that has handed down the final sentence must issue a statement on whether there is reason to recommend the convicted person for clemency. The execution will be postponed if the convicted person becomes insane.

That meant that the death penalty could, in theory, still be upheld during times of war, though this was extended to the Danish Folketing (Government).

In the 1990s, discussions started on whether the Faroe Islands should be included in the new Danish Military Act from 1973, which abolished Denmark's death penalty during the war. This was part of a so-called "Ríkislógartilmæli," a recommendation concerning the Kingdom of Realm. But in 1992, the Faroese Government declared it unsuitable to remove the Military Act only to introduce a new Danish law in the Faroe Islands.

---

1. The King, in Danish law, is interpreted as the Danish Government.

The recommendation to abolish the 1937 Military Act was put forth again in the early 2000s. On the 22nd of November 2001, the Military Act of 1937 was removed without any opposing vote, though it was without adopting the 1973 law. An official statement was sent to the Danish Ministry of Justice on the 4th of December 2001, and the death penalty was now entirely abolished. Or so they thought.

The Faroe Islands even took a step further and discussed declaring the *European Convention on Human Rights*, which, according to Protocol No. 13, abolishes the death penalty in all circumstances. This was adopted on the 21st of February 2002. But, as it turned out, the letter sent to the Ministry of Justice was nowhere to be found, and in March 2003, the 1937 Military Act was still not cancelled; therefore, the death penalty was still part of the Faroese regulation. It was then agreed to send another letter to Denmark to resolve these matters, and later the same year, the law was formally abolished.

Chapter Four

Religion and Superstition

The Beliefs of the Faroe Islands

The Faroe Islands is a very religious country. Approximately 80% are part of the State Church, while another 10% are affiliated with the free churches, whilst the other 10% either subscribe to other religions or are atheists. Even though people are leaving the church, now more than ever, the population growth sustains these numbers. This means that the number of churchgoers is steadily increasing, although the number of people leaving the church is increasing too.

The Faroe Islands are way more religious than the other Nordic countries. Studies within religion have shown that if one should find another country comparable with the Faroe Islands, one must look to the United States of America, the country in the Western world most comparable to the Faroes regarding religiosity.

With religiosity comes a traditional worldview, and it likely isn't surprising that Faroese people tend to be quite conservative, as this highly correlates with religious beliefs. However, in recent years, there has been a minor cultural revolution where young people have rejected the conservative ways and replaced them with more modern ideas, which historically have not been widespread in the Faroes. With influence from neighbouring countries, globalisation, and trends accessible on the internet, the Faroe Islands have become more liberal than they have ever been. This can be seen in the legislation in 2016 that legalised same-sex marriages and, in 2019, made child adoptions legal for same-sex couples.

Saksun Church. Photo by Timo Kornelsen on Pexels.

The current debate is focusing much on women's rights and the question of abortion, and like with the questions of same-sex marriages and the right to adopt for same-sex couples, the debates and discussions have been ongoing, with strong opinions and organisations advocating either side.

It is often stated that the Faroe Islands is a Christian nation, and even though the Faroes have no legislation saying that it is, some legislation, like the legislation regarding public schools, states that schools must give students a moral Christian upbringing.

The First Christians

The first settlers of the Faroe Islands were Christian monks believed to have sought solitude in Iceland and the Faroe Islands. Not much is known about these monks, except that they were from Ireland and that they were Christians, which is well documented in historical Irish documents. As suggested by the placenames, which can be found across the islands, the Viking settlers and the Irish monks did encounter each other. Still, what happened to the monks or whether they influenced the Norwegian invaders' belief system is unknown.

In the Færeyinga Saga, it is said that the Viking chieftain Sigmundur Brestisson brought Christianity to the islands in the year 1000. Because of this, many believe the Saga to be true, although the historical reliability is questionable.

Excavations across the country have revealed Christian symbols in several Viking villages, although other religious symbols, some Celtic, have also been found. This suggests a connection between the Faroes, Britain, and Ireland, although it isn't clear how this might have influenced the beliefs of the first Faroe islanders. The same connection is evident in the Faroese genome, which shows Norwegian and Irish descent.

By 1.100, the Christian religion was well established, and the church had its seating in Kirkjubø, which became a stronghold for the church and king.

Although not much has been documented from the first years of the church, folktales that have been surpassed by oral tradition mention the church and how it was seen as an oppressive institution collecting high taxes for establishing churches around the country, especially in Kirkjubø. This eventually led to a civil war between people from the north and the south. The civil war happened around 1300 and is partly supported by Norwegian sources of the time.

Although the Faroe Islands had been Roman Catholic for around 500 years, they became Lutheran during the rule of the last bishop of the Faroes, Jens Riber, who was bishop from 1540 to 1556. Since then, the Lutheran faith has been the dominant faith in the Faroe Islands.

Free Churches

The second largest Christian affiliation is the Brethren Movement. In the late 1800s, it came to the Faroes from the Plymouth Baptist Church, which originated in southern England. Compared to the church, it was received as a miniature Christian revolution that broke from many of its traditions. Now, it was possible to use other instruments during sermons, and Christian meetings were often held in nature, with people being baptised in lakes, rivers, and even the sea.

However, the Brethren also introduced a new perception of sin because while Faroese superstition and tradition had always coexisted with the Christian faith, some practices were now seen as sinful. Brethren were not allowed to participate in the Faroese chain dance, and trick-or-treating during Easter was also considered a sin.

Biblical texts and psalms were translated into Faroese. The Brethren movement played a significant role in developing written Faroese and using the Faroese language in general. The translations were extensive, and with the primary goal of making the Christian message accessible to regular people, they were much easier to read. Here, missionary Victor Danielsen (b. 1894 - d. 1961) translated 800 Psalms, 18 books, and the Bible.

Today, there are many different free evangelic churches, many of which have strong ties to Christian movements in the United States of America. At the same time, other religious institutions like the Morman Church and Scientology have not been introduced yet. Even though Jews and Muslims live on the Faroes, there are no Jewish synagogues or Muslim mosques.

The Folk-belief

In the olden days, people used to believe in ferries, pixies, hidden people (a form of elves), dwarfs, trolls, giants, mermaids, selkies, kelpies, nightmares, and dwarfs. Today, these beliefs can be considered gone, but as late as the early 1900s, belief in different kinds of ghosts and people having special abilities was common. Some still hold these beliefs as accurate, but it can no longer be said that they are part of any popular belief.

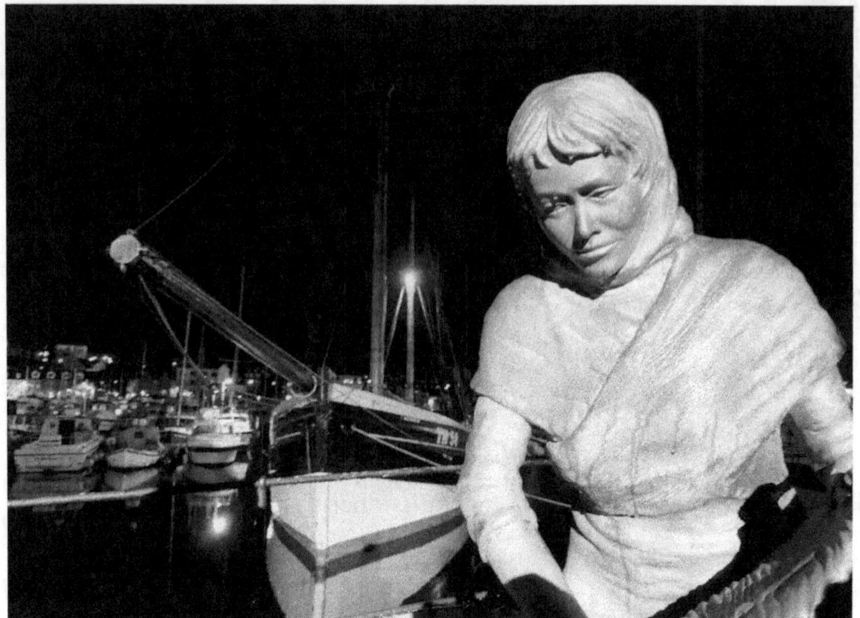

Statue of a Faroese woman and a wooden shcooner. Photo by Rúni í Múla.

Often, it is said that the trolls disappeared with the electricity. That is partly true because when houses were modernised with modern kitchens, the social gatherings in the evenings that used to be an integral part of everyday life disappeared. At these social gatherings, people sang songs and told stories—many of which were stories about the supernatural.

Back then, people used to believe in all sorts of mythical beings, which, to them, were as accurate as their belief in God. But, even though superstitious beliefs and Christianity often are seen as counter opposites, the two sets of beliefs co-existed.

In the Faroese interpretation of Christianity, nothing prohibited these two world views from existing simultaneously; instead, they were entwined with the belief in God, who was used to protect the dangerous creatures living amongst them. This is evident in some of the magic spells that have survived through time, where the name of God has been part of protection spells, and many of the supernatural beings that were part of the folk-belief were highly sensitive to the name of God or the sight of churches, and so forth.

Even though most of the superstitious beliefs have vanished, they are not entirely gone, as some still hold beliefs in certain things such as ghosts while the belief in trolls and hidden people must be considered extinct. However, the stories and the old beliefs continue to influence the Faroese art scene to this day, which is evident in music, fine arts, and in litterature.

Chapter Five

The Language and the Nobel Prize

Recognition in One Way or Another

Although the Faroese language is closely related to the Old Norse language and is ancient, the Faroese written language is only a little over 150 years old. Faroese people could read and write in the Viking Age, as some of the country's oldest documents suggest. Still, the written language fell into the background over time and disappeared completely in the early Middle Ages.

Under the Danish king, it was mandated that Danish be used in the church and schools. The Faroe Islands were then considered a Danish County because, at that time, they were considered part of Denmark, similar to places like Bornholm and Southern Jutland.

Danish was considered finer than Faroese, and it was even claimed that God could not understand Faroese. Therefore, parts of the Faroese upper class insisted on speaking Danish instead of Faroese for several generations. But even though Faroese could not be accommodated in either the school or the church, the language has survived among the ordinary people, even if, by all the world's standards, it must be considered an endangered language, which a very limited population has only used. However, the language has always been in active use, which may have been the reason for the language's survival.

A Written Language is Born

In 1781 - 1782, the priest Jens Christian Svabo travelled in the Faroe Islands. He made an extensive collection of Faroese words and texts on his journey. But since there was no written language, he had to create his own language himself - this effort became the first bid for a reconstructed written language. Still, even though he made this effort, he was convinced that Danish had influenced the Faroese so much that the language would not survive over time. But Svabo's great effort meant that others were inspired to make similar collections.

In the 1820s, the first books were published in Faroese. These were ballads, biblical texts and the Færeyinga saga, translated by the priest Jóhan Hendrik Schrøter, also published in a language that was another attempt at a Faroese written language. However, some years passed before the Faroese written language was reborn. In 1846, the priest Venceslaus Ulricus Hammershaimb introduced a common written language, which he had constructed with the great help of linguistic scholars from Denmark and Iceland. Instead of using a phonetic form, this language was based on the oldest forms of the language, with inspiration from Icelandic words and German grammar. With some adaptations, this became the language we know today as the written Faroese language.

Portrait of V. U. Hammershaimb. Photo by Niels Christian Hansen and Frantz Clemens Stephan Weller. Det Kgl. Bibliotek.

However, the language was much debated, and the recognition of the language took many years until it was finally recognised among the Faroese. One of the language's critics was Dr Jakob Jakobsen, who had also done much collecting work. He believed that the language was too complicated to use and that a phonetic writing system would be more accessible for ordinary people to learn and use. He presented his proposal for a Faroese written language, but this caused great anger among those who were supporters of Hammershaimb's spelling and ended up not being adopted. However, books were also published in Jakobsen Faroese at this time.

It was only in 1938 that Faroese became part of the curriculum in primary schools, and in 1939, Faroese was accepted in the churches.

William Heinesen and the Nobel Prize

William Heinesen (b. 15th of January 1900 - d. 12th of March 1991) was a Faroese author, composer, and artist.

He was born and raised in the Faroe Islands, where he lived most of his life except for some years when he was young. He wrote in Danish as this was the language he had been taught at home and in school. Therefore, the books he published were originally all written in Danish.

In his time, he was considered one of the most influential writers in Danish, and for that, he was considered to be nominated for the Nobel Prize in Literature in 1977.

In addition to his literary work, Heinesen is considered among the all-time best artists from the Faroes. His works mainly revolve around Faroese myth and folklore. He was a pronounced art critic in the artistic subculture, and many have drawn inspiration from his creative paintings and works.

Chapter Six
Cartology and the Faroes
Floating Islands and Fictive Countries

I t is relatively common to see modern maps that do not include the Faroe Islands. This is the case both in physical and electronic maps. The Faroe Islands have had significant issues with shipping because the Faroe Islands are not included on several websites that supposedly ship worldwide. When it comes to large corporations such as Google, it has also been a challenge to get the Faroe Islands included in Google Maps, which, however, was made possible by a campaign by the Faroese tourist bureau, Visit Faroe Islands, after the campaign known as *Sheep View*.

However, the Faroe Islands are very tiny, and the political landscape of not being a sovereign state while still having self-rule doesn't help in the general international recognition. Therefore, it is understandable by most that people out in the world haven't heard of the islands, and consequently, it is also understandable that the peninsula gets left out on some of the world's maps out there. But, even though this is something that keeps recurring, the Faroe Islands do appear on some of the maps stemming from the Middle Ages.

Frislandia

In the so-called Zeno map, a map of the North Atlantic Ocean from around 1400 made by the Italian brothers Nicolò and Antonio Zeno, there is an island to the West of the Faroe Islands. The island is called Frislandia and has either never existed or been mistaken for some of the existing islands in the North Atlantic.

The brothers claimed to have been on a voyage in the 1390s and had supposedly spent some time on the island of Frisland. Archival documents do, however, suggest that the Zeno brothers were in Venice, Italy, when their journey up north was said to have taken place, and today, the Zeno map is being considered a hoax by most scholars.

When Nicolò Zeno published the map, it was widely accepted as accurate. Because of cartologists' method of producing maps of the world then, the island of Frisland appeared on virtually all maps from the 1560s to the 1660s.

Those who believe the Zeno brothers' claimed journey have debated whether the island of Frisland has been a forgery or if the brothers mistook it for Iceland, Southern Greenland, Northern Scotland, the Shetland Islands, or the Faroe Islands. At different times, these countries have all claimed to be the one country depicted as Frisland.

Frisland (1500s). Map by Antonio Lafréry.

A case can be made that the Zeno brothers did mistake Frisland for the southern part of the Faroes because of the people who lived there around the same time as the brothers. During the 1400s, on the southernmost part of the Faroe Islands, legend tells of a Frisian colony (from Germany or the Netherlands) living in and around the area today known as Akraberg. These people lived separately from the rest of the Faroe Islanders and had distinct cultures. The legends surrounding these Frisians are all presumed to be from around 1300 and 1350, though some believe they have lived there since 700 or 800. If, say, the Zeno brothers visited this part of the Faroe Islands in the 1390s, it is plausible that they have met some of those who had survived the Black Plague that ravaged the Faroes in the mid-1300s, and which is said to have extinguished most of the Frisians. If that were the case, that would explain the name Frislandia.

However, the Frisian colonists are believed to have moved north because of political disputes in Germany and the Netherlands, leading them to the Faroes, the British Isles, Scandinavia, and Iceland. Therefore, the Zeno brothers might have encountered the Frisian people elsewhere.

Floating Islands

There are many legends surrounding the islands of the Faroe Islands. Many of them are said to have been floating islands which have been floating about in the North Atlantic Ocean. In the days of the priest Lucas Debes (b. 1623 - d. 1675), floating islands were still believed to exist, which is evident in one of the passages in his book Færoæ & Færoæ Reserata from 1673 where he writes of an account where a ship had passed an island in the south-east of the Faroes. In those waters, there was no known island, and the crew on the ship believed that island to be a floating island. Reading

Debes' reflections, although he is sceptical of floating islands, he was undoubtedly entertaining the idea. In his reflections on this stated account, he reflects on icebergs drifting from the North Pole and on another island, Enckhuyser Eyland, discovered near Iceland by the Dutch, which has since disappeared and which people also believed to be a floating island.

Of the Faroese islands, Fugloy, Svínoy, and Mykines are all said to have been floating islands that aimlessly drifted through the Atlantic Ocean before they were attached to the seabed in the Faroe Islands. Skúvoy is also said to have been a floating island, but the legend connected to this story has sadly been forgotten.

Chapter Seven

Animal Life

Extinction and Nearly Extinction

When the Vikings first arrived in the Faroes, the islands had a rich birdlife, and sheep and horses were already living on the islands. No one knows how these animals first came to the islands. Still, the original Faroese sheep breed is believed to be closely related to the breed that lives on Soay in the Outer Hebrides in Scotland, and the horse breed is closely related to the Shetland Pony. Therefore, it is believed that the first domestic animals arrived in the Faroes by the Irish monks, though they could have been brought by the people who were on the islands a few hundred years earlier, which nothing is known about.

In this chapter, I will introduce some of the most interesting stories and explanations of animals from the islands. But I have decided not to include other animals, such as the Faroese duck and the Faroese chicken, because close to nothing is written about these animals, and they still need to be investigated to determine whether they are a Faroese breed, as many do believe.

The Faroese Horse

The Faroese horse is a small type of horse whose origin is unknown. Some believe they arrived with the Viking settlements, while others believe they were brought to the Faroes with the Irish monks who settled on the islands some hundred years before. In the 1950s, a Scottish veterinarian, James Speed, researched the breed and concluded that the breed originated from the breed that was common in North Scotland until the year 850 when a law was set in action which prohibited people from eating horse meat. Because of this law, the north Scottish breed was exported to Iceland and the Faroe Islands. This explanation seems plausible, but it is the only research that has been done on the topic.

In 1987, the Danish advisor on horse breeding, Henning Rasmussen, wrote the following description:

"The Faroese horse is a small, harmonious and attractive horse (pony) with relative depth and width. It has a well-shaped dry and expressive head. Mostly a little short, but well-set neck. The shoulder and mane area form a good saddle bearing. It has a strong topline, muscular and well-shaped - regularly a little short - croup and good thigh muscles. The limbs are relatively leaden and dry and predominantly fit, but a French pretence occurs. Throughout its knee and hocks are well marked and the breed has extremely good hooves with good horn quality. The movement is predominantly energetic and light. The Faroese

horse is known as a very enduring horse that can carry a relatively large weight and is also very safe on its feet."

In the 1800s, around 800 individual horses lived on the Faroe Islands, mainly used for everyday work. From 1850 to 1900, the horses had a high selling value and were sold to Great Britain to work in the coal mine industry. Their small size and incredible strength made them perfect for the coal industry as they were used to shove the coal wagons in the mines. When most of the horses were sold off, there was simultaneously an increasing interest among the Faroe Islanders in importing new horse breeds, which people found much more desirable than the original horse. This made selling the Faroese horses even worse for the species that used to populate the islands. Eventually, nearly no pure breeds were left, and the horses were ultimately believed to be extinct. From this, some say that the saying "to make a horse trade" (i.e., a temporary advantage which in the long term proves to be a disadvantage) originates and refers to the unsustainable trades which almost ended up making the breed entirely extinct. This saying is, however, well-known in other languages, and there is no reason to believe that this saying has anything to do with the selling off of Faroese horses, even though it fits.

In the 1960s, people started to get interested in the horse again, but believing they were extinct, people tried looking to see if they could find any horses left that no one knew about. When they started looking, they found only five individuals, of whom only one was male. Three of the female horses were descendants of the fourth female horse, an old mare from the island of Vágar. The people who had led the investigation now saw that if the horses were to survive, they had to act instantly.

A Faroese horse near Gásadalur. Photo by Maria Teneva on Unsplash.

Today, the Faroese Pony is still endangered and has only 87 individual horses (numbers from 2023). The local association, *Føroyska Rossið*, the Faroese Horse, and *Felagið Føroysk Ross*, The Faroese Horse Association, is working to sustain the population. Still, there are great worries about its endangerments and specific traits that only a few horses have, which derive from a particular genome that is hard to breed. Unfortunately, the association has pressured politicians who have not called for action.

Political passivity has led interest organizations to take new paths. In 2024, they exported semen and eggs, which were put into a female horse in Denmark, with the hope of starting horse breeding outside the Faroe Islands and strengthening the population. Selection and mating of horses is done with a genome program that ensures the least possible inbreeding, which helps to increase the chances of the horse breed's survival.

The Faroese Cow

It is believed that the Faroese cow was brought to the islands with the first settlers. No one knows whether it was the Irish monks or the Norwegian Vikings, but it is believed to be of Norwegian descent, which indicates that it most likely was brought by the Vikings. The Faroese cow was, however, its own breed, and like the horse, it was smaller than cattle from the neighbouring countries.

aroese politician and poet Rasmus Effersøe was the first to describe the breed. He described it as small, short-legged, with short horns, and mainly black.

When milk machines were introduced in the Faroe Islands, modern machines were not suited for small cows. Therefore, farmers started cross-breeding the cattle by importing them from Denmark, Iceland, Norway, and the United Kingdom. In 1987, some specimens that hadn't been crossbred were still left, but Hestur was the only island with bulls. Instead of preserving the original species, the cattle were introduced to specimens from Norway, and after that, none of the original cattle was ever born again.

Farmers were happy because the crossbreeding was so effective that it doubled the cow's milk.

In 2003, all cattle on the islands were inspected in search of the original species. From around 1,000 cows, eight specimens seemed to closely resemble the original breed, though it was evident that these had been crossed with other breeds. In hopes of conserving the remaining original genes, genome samples were collected and preserved for further investigation. With the genome, scientists hope to be able to reintroduce cattle more closely related to the original Faroese cow.

With the 2003 investigation, it was finally evident that the Faroese cow had, in fact, gone extinct.

The Sheep of Dímun

The sheep known as the Dímunarseyður —the Sheep of Dímun—was the original breed of sheep that roamed the islands before the Norse Viking settlers arrived in the Faroes between the late 6th and late 8th centuries.

The sheep was a primitive short-tailed breed closely related to the sheep that live on the island of Soay in St. Kilda in the Outer Hebrides of Scotland. The sheep had short wool, which was not suited for knitting. Therefore, the islanders only learned knitting after introducing the breed of sheep that live on the islands today, presented in the 1600s.

The sheep survived on the island of Dímun while being extinct throughout the rest of the islands, and therefore, it was named after the island. Being isolated for so long, the sheep had become wild and hostile towards people, and when people from Hvalba and Sanvdík in Suðuroy bought the island in 1850, the remaining sheep were shot. This was because the sheep were hard to capture, and men felt frightened of being rammed by the sheep and off the island's steep cliffs.

Two male sheep of the new sheep breed. Photo by Kasper Lau on Unsplash.

From some local legends in Sandoy, which have been written down in the 1970s, it is said that the sheep there sometimes have been hard to handle and have shown to be quite aggressive. It has, therefore, been believed that these sheep had interbred with the original breed of the island and that the sheep of Sandoy shared some of the genes of the Dímunarseyður.

Whether or not this is true, no one knows. The sheep breed that lives on the islands today all share some of the genes of the old breed. However, there are some indications that the sheep of Sandoy might be more inbred with the original species, as indicated by the old sheepfolds there. Unlike in other places throughout the islands, these sheepfolds have been partly dug into the ground, making a hole to trap the sheep in when the sheep are driven into the fold. That way, it is more difficult for the sheep to escape than in any regular sheepfold.

The White Raven

The White-Pied Raven, Hvítravnur, was a white-pigmented raven that used to live in the Faroe Islands. It was the same race as the black ravens that live on the islands today, but due to a gene malfunction, the pigments had changed for some of them, which turned their colour white and brown. The pied raven was only found on the Faroe Islands, even though the breed was closely related to the North Atlantic species.

Like the Faroese horse, people abroad became eager to get their hands on the pied raven. Prices for stuffed examples were high, so they were in high demand.

The White Pied Raven. Illustration by John Gerrard Keulemans.

Before and during the spiked interest for this bird, a system ordered anyone to deliver the beaks of ravens and eagles once a year towards payment. This was to control the population of these birds that were harmful to young sheep, especially in the spring, and had a considerable impact on the food resources upon which the islanders depended. This system eventually ended the sea eagle, which was nesting in a few hard-to-reach places in the country, but the pied raven was so common that its population was not considered threatened. The interest in Europe, however, caused the last white raven to be shot in 1902; some examples were seen after that, and the last one was seen in 1948.

Whales and Whaling

One cannot talk about animals in the Faroe Islands without mentioning whales and the controversial whale-hunting tradition known as the grind.

The Faroese have hunted whales since before Faroese history was recorded, though it is mentioned in the Sheep Letter from 1298. It is most likely a tradition that goes as far back as Viking times, but statistics have been made from each whale hunt since 1584, the oldest unbroken statistic in the world.

The whales being hunted are primarily pilot whales and sometimes also North Atlantic dolphins. The hunt itself involves only the pods of whales that swim between the islands—whalers do not go to sea to search for whales. When fishing vessels sail by a pod of whales, they are not driven towards the shores.

The whale hunt is a bloody affair, as one might imagine when such large animals are slaughtered in the free and sea. Whales are large and contain a lot of blood; therefore, the sea gets red during the slaughter.

But though it might be dramatic, the slaughter is perceived as a natural part of life, and it is common to see children participate in the slaughter; this is not a harmful or traumatising experience for the children.

In recent years, the Faroe Islands have experienced increased pressure from animal welfare activists, who have tried to put a full stop to the whale hunt but without succeeding. Some activist organisations have been known to use rather extreme methods to stop the grind by making one-sided documentaries, which, to the Faroese, have been perceived as dishonest and disrupting the hunt using speed boats. In fact, during one of these attempts, crew members from the organisation Sea Shepherd were fined for animal cruelty because the propeller of their speed boats had sliced up several whales when they were sailing back and forth to disrupt the whale hunt.

However, the focus on animal welfare has also impacted methods used for slaughter; some tools have been banned, and some new tools have been invented. In only a few years, a unique spear was developed, which paralyses the whale instantly by piercing it into the whale's blow hole, making the killing more humane. Also, since 2013, anyone who participates in a whale slaughter must have a licence, which one can get by attending a whale slaughtering course.

The whaling tradition is a solidary system in which anyone who participates gets their share of the catch. Sometimes, everyone from a village also gets their share of the catch.

Due to heavy metal pollution, fewer and fewer young people eat whale meat. Whale meat is not recommended as food for young people of fertile age by the authorities, as mercury pollution settles in the body and can be inherited by newborns. At the same time, some young people distance themselves from whaling, as many are against meat production by being vegan or vegetarian.

Chapter Eight

Challenging Delicacies

Potatoes, Something Rotten and Potatoes Again

To a foreigner, the Faroese kitchen must be rather extreme. It's hard to talk about culture without mentioning the food associated with it. Due to the lack of agriculture and the wet climate, the Faroes have developed some peculiar food traditions using conservation methods that are quite different from those of the rest of Europe.

In the olden days, before refrigerators, there were only a few ways to preserve food that had been caught. Meat and fish were preserved using either salt or drying methods for fermentation, using the wind and the wet climate.

Fermented Faroese food has a strong smell and a strong taste. Though it might be an acquired taste, most Faroese people perceive these kinds of food as special delicacies, and to anyone who hasn't tried it, it is certainly an experience that you cannot have anywhere else in the world.

Fisherman handling whale meat. Photo by Robert Bahn on Unsplash.

The Faroese cold and wet climate with a stable temperature throughout the year makes for optimal conditions for fermenting meat and fish. Traditionally, this kind of food is served with beer and aquavit (a Scandinavian kind of spirit) but it is excellent with sea-infused single malt whiskey, such as Talisker Whiskey or other kinds of whiskeys from the Scottish coastline or islands.

Roots and potatoes

In the olden days, when the Faroe Islands was still a Danish County, the King demanded that all farmers pay their taxes using corn stock. But as the weather on the Faroe Islands was cold, wet, and harsh, the farmers struggled to grow their crops. It was possible to grow corn, but it was very ineffective, and the farmers struggled to get enough stock to pay what they owed to the King.

Farmers could use their land much more efficiently with the introduction of potatoes. Just as it did in Ireland, it changed what the farmers could deliver in taxes to the King because while the corn was tough to manage, the potatoes were much easier to maintain and seemed to flourish in the Faroese climate.

The first documented potato was in 1686, and the way it is mentioned suggests that it was common at that point. It is believed that roots were introduced simultaneously. When the potato was first introduced, it became prevalent, and soon, potato fields were a common sight around the islands. In some places, one can see how the people have cleared the mountainsides for potato harvesting and removed entire mountains for rocks and stones.

If there is anything that defines any traditional Faroese dish, it is the potato. No matter what recipe, it will most likely contain potatoes.

Salted food

One food-preserving method is salt. It is common to have a large barrel in the drying sheds with whale meat and blubber; some also have such barrels with fish.

In the olden days, making salted fish and exporting it primarily to Spain was common. Here, it is said that the Faroese brought the Bacalao tradition to Spain, though this idea has yet to be confirmed. If that is true, then the Spaniards must be said to have experimented with and evolved it because, in the Faroes, salted fish is typically served in the same way as it has always been with potatoes and sweet-sour sauce.

Fermented food

Ræst kjøt and *ræstur fiskur* are two Faroese delicacies distinct in taste and smell. Ræst kjøt is fermented sheep meat and ræstur fiskur is fermented fish. Even though it isn't as common as it used to be, whale meat, primarily the ribs, is sometimes also fermented.

Fermentation is a rotting process that preserves food by handing it up to dry. In other cultures, we know fermentation from preserving vegetables like kimchi and sauerkraut. In the Faroes, however, it has traditionally been fish or meat when something is fermented.

The meat is dried in a drying shed with barred walls where the wind can blow through. This keeps the meat away from the rain while it is dried over a long period by the salty breeze. When the food is ready, it has a strong smell and a solid aromatic taste, which many tourists have often found off-putting. However, the locals love it and associate it with the festive seasons.

Dried fermented fish. Photo by Dan Mall on Unsplash.

Chapter Nine

Alcohol Ban or Liberalisation

Social Strains and Endless Disputes

The Faroe Islands have always had an ambivalent relationship with alcohol. This is evident each time proposals are made for amendments to the alcohol law and presented for the political system. The reason can be found in a part of Faroese history that has not yet been exceptionally well researched and still arouses strong opposing feelings in many people.

Although the Faroe Islands has a well-regulated system today, it has not always been that way.

A History of Monopoly

In 1271, when the Faroe Islands were still part of Norway, the Norwegian king introduced the Monopoly Store, a complete and closed system in which all legal trade to and from the Faroes had to occur exclusively. When the Faroe Islands became part of the Danish kingdom, the monopoly store continued similarly, with all trades connected to the Danish king. However, in 1855, the monopoly store was demolished, and this was the first time in 584 years that the Faroe Islands had free trade.

With the dissolution of the monopoly store, trade became more accessible and cheaper, and at first, this seemed like groundbreaking progress for the Faroese Islands. Now, all trade was free, and people got better deals by selling and buying their goods. However, the new opportunities were not all positive, as they brought along unforeseen downsides that would shock the Faroese society to its core and cause societal problems so severe that they would affect generations to come.

A Society in Shambles

Life in the Faroe Islands has always been difficult, and it has always required hard work, both at work and at home. Whether these conditions impacted the developing alcohol culture, one can only guess. But already, at the start of free trade, it was clear that the Faroese consumed excessive alcohol.

Binge drinking became normal among men, and many started drinking so heavily that they would spend all their hard-earned money on alcohol. This affected their families so severely that they could not afford to pay their bills, and they did not have money for either food or warm clothes. There were many tragic fates. Families that had otherwise been well-functioning ended up in deep poverty. This was especially true for those who, after having spent all their salary, started gambling their next month's salary or were even gambling using their property. This resulted in many drinking away their land, properties that had been within the families for generations, and for some, even their homes. This created a long series of social problems, which were also taken very seriously among the rest of the sober population, mainly consisting of women and people with a background in religious movements that had also begun to be introduced to society.

People Take Action

In 1884, a public meeting was held in Tórshavn, where all champions of the fight against alcohol met. Also at the meeting was Djóni í Geil, who was one of the founders of the Faroe Islands' first abstinence association and one of the leading figures in the movement who continued to work to anchor the abstinence associations around the country. At the meeting, he suggested that all the local abstinence associations join together and publish a newspaper to support their work and goals in the fight against alcohol. The newspaper was to be distributed throughout the country and inform about the damage caused by consuming too much alcohol and about the activities of the associations. The proposal did not go through.

In the years that followed, more and more abstinence associations were established nationwide, and among the leading figures in the work was Djóni í Geil. 10 years later, in 1894, when the associations had gained a better footing, the proposal became a reality, and the temperance newspaper Dúgvan was established. At this time, Djóni í Geil was chairman of the abstinence association in Tórshavn and was appointed newspaper editor.

Dúgvan was published once a month and played a significant role in informing about the social damage alcohol consumption had on the Faroe Islands. These were part of the reasons why Djóni í Geil was named an honorary member of the women's abstinence association in Tórshavn.

The organised abstinence movement changed the view on alcohol and created a strong identity for entire settlements, which proudly and honourably proclaimed themselves abstinence settlements. Some of these abstinence settlements still exist today, while in other places, the movement still echoes.

In addition, the movement also changed the political debate, where politicians began to consider how alcohol should be regulated. But the politicians acted late, and the abstinence associations pressed on. During this period, there was a large influx of women in the associations, who now produced demands that alcohol should be totally banned.

The proposal was put forward in 1906, but as women had yet to be given the right to vote, they and the abstinence community demanded that the proposal be put to a referendum and that the women be given the right to vote to be heard. In 1907, a referendum was held, and for the first time, women had the right to vote. The result was that distilled alcohol production and brewing of strong beer was made illegal.

DÚGVAN.

UDKOMMER
1 GANG
HVER MAANED.

ABONNEMENTSPRIS
1 KR.
PR. AAR.

AFHOLDSBLAD FOR FÆRØERNE.

UDGIVET AF FÆLLESUDVALGET FOR FÆRØSKE AFHOLDSORGANISATIONER.

| Nr. 8. | AUGUST 1916. | 23. Aarg. |

DIONE ISAKSEN.

F. 12. septembur 1849. — D. 20. april 1912.

Um ólavsøkutíðir í árinum 1885 var í Havn hildin ein fundur, hvar meginparturin av teimum, ið stóðu fremst í stríðinum móti rúsdrekkanum, var komin tilstaðar. Djóni í Geil bar á hesum fundi fram uppskot um at geva út eitt avhaldsblað fyri Føroyar. Øll vóru samsint í ti, at henda sak átti at fremjast, so skjótt tað á nakran hátt var gjørligt at fáa tilvegis tann pening, ið tørvaðist til at útinna hetta endamál. Ikki fyrr enn 9 ár seinni vóru líkindini so tolulig, at farast kundi undir at fremja áðurnevnda uppskot, soleiðis at avhaldsblaðið »Dúgvan« frá 1. januar 1894 kundi byrja at flúgva út um Føroyaland. »Dúgvan« varð givin út av »Havnar avhaldsfelag« við Djóna í Geil sum blaðstýrara. Frá 1894 til 1908 var Djóni blaðstýrari, fárroknað o. n. eitt árstíð (1900—1901), tá Rasmus Effersøe skrivaði »Dúgvuna«. Vegna heilsuloysi segði Djóni seg í 1908 frá sum blaðstýrari, og »Dúgvan« varð givin arbeiðsnevnd »Havnar avhaldsfelag« upp í hendur.

Tó at »Dúgvan« var lítið blað, og bert kom út eina ferð um mánaðin, gjørdi Djóni her eitt arbeiði av ómetuliga stórum týdningi fyri land og fólk. Í 13 ár skrivaði hann so at siga púra einsamallur blaðið, utan at fáa eitt oyra aftur fyri; tíðum varð blaðið hildið fyri spott og illa viðfarið av mótstøðumonnum; vánaliga gekkst at fáa haldarar, og av teimum, ið høvdu teknað seg fyri blaðið, fullu nógvir frá aftur. Eitt avhaldsblað kundi sjálvsagt ikki bera seg her í Føroyum, og tí mátti »Havnar avhaldsfelag« ferð eftir ferð stýðja tað við peningi. Undir slíkum viðurskiftum var tað eitt torført arbeiði at royna at halda liv í hesum blað, tolin og áhaldandi mátti hann vera, ið stóð á odda í hesum strevi.

Djóni í Geil.

Í 42 ár stóð Djóni í Geil sum ein av teim fremstu undangongumonnum og slóðbrótarum í øllum avhaldsarbeiði í Føroyum. Saman við C. C. Danielsen og Eliaser Andreasen stovnaði hann hitt fyrsta føroyska avhaldsfelagið, sum tó bert livdi í 4 ár. Stutt aftaná oyddnaðist tað tó teim somu monnum at fáa íbirt »Havnar avhaldsfelag«, sum nú brátt er 38 ára gamalt.

Tá C. C. Danielsen segði seg frá sum formaður fyri »Havnar avhaldsfelag«, var Djóni í Geil valgdur til formans; ár undan ári varð hann afturvalgdur, líka til heilsuloysi noyddi hann at siga seg frá.

Við at íbirta avhaldsfelag víða hvar í føroyskum bygdum og eftir førimuni royna at halda liv í hesum feløgum, gjørdi Djóni í Geil eitt stórt og munagott arbeiði fyri avhaldssakina í Føroyum. Hann var við til at stovna »Havnar kvinnu-avhaldsfelag«, og fyri tann stuðul og ta velvild, hann hevði víst hesi fyritøku, útnevndu kvinnurnar hann til heiðurslim av teirra felag. Hann var eisini heiðurslimur av »Havnar avhaldsfelag«. Djóni í Geil var barnavinur sum fáir; honum dámdi sera væl at tosa við børnini og greiða teimum frá tí vanlukku, rúsdrekkanjótan førdi við sær. Hann íbirti í Havnini eitt barna-avhaldsfelag, og so leingi hann hevði heilsuna og orkaði at strevast fyri hesum felag við samkomum, útferðum og tílíkum, treivst tað sera væl. Í hesum arbeiði varð Djóni væl styðjaður av Chr. Christiansen (undir ryggi).

Í øll tey ár, Djóni í Geil var formaður fyri »Havnar avhaldsfelag«, var hann eisini odlamaður í strevinum fyri at fáa í lag bønarbrøv frá tí føroyska avhaldsfólkinum til løgtingið viðvíkjandi rúsdrekkalóggeving.

Djóni í Geil. Article and Picture by Dúgvan.

New Restrictions Forced a "Gatherer" Mentality

The new alcohol law of 1907 was the first attempt to limit access to alcohol. Although the abstinence associations advocated for a complete ban, politicians sympathised with the breweries, which had already been hard hit by the strict rules. Therefore, it was decided that the breweries could only brew beer with a maximum alcohol percentage of 4.6%, while they had to completely stop distilling.

However, alcohol was still legal to consume, and therefore a trade agreement was established with a dealer in Denmark who was responsible for importing alcohol to the Faroe Islands.For the first time, the political system had been given a tool to be able to regulate intake and the market. This became evident in 1928, when new restrictions intertwined the right to buy alcohol with the tax-paying system. With these changes, you could only buy alcohol if you had paid off all your taxes and were debt-free towards the government.

The craving for alcohol was great, and politically, people were cautious in regulating consumption too much. The restrictions were calculated per quarter, where you could order a maximum of 9 litres of spirits with an alcohol content of 23% or less and 9 litres with an alcohol content of 23% or more. Beer was even less regulated, although you could buy a maximum of 42 litres of beer per month.

Although these regulations sound like massive amounts of alcohol, people were afraid of having too little. This led to people ordering as much as they could each quarter. Even so, a trend among men was found to have drunk everything before the three months had passed.

The hypothesis for this behaviour is that because people knew there was a limit to how much they could order, they always tried to order as much as possible to ensure they never ran out of a drink.

A Call for Reformation

In 1936, a new alcohol law was proposed. The idea was to introduce a Faroese monopoly store, which handled all alcohol sales. But people still remembered how things were when alcohol was a free trade product, and the law proposal fell and would leave the political discussions for many years. A similar proposal was put forth in 1973 and was accepted by the then-ruling government, though it had to go through a referendum before it could go into action. The referendum was held, and once again, the proposal was rejected.

In 1980, the strong "Giraffe" and "Elephant" beers were banned, and the alcohol limit of 4.6% was increased to 5.7%. This was the first time since the alcohol ban in 1907 that the law was liberalised.

In 1991, the proposal to establish a monopoly store for alcohol was reintroduced, with an extensive hearing process conducted by all of society's relevant stakeholders. Once again, it stirred a comprehensive debate. But on March 10, 1992, the law was finally accepted, and the monopoly store, Rúsan, was established.

Since introducing the new monopoly store, Rúsan, the government has kept statistics on alcohol consumption. As it turns out, each time the law has been made less restrictive, and as the monopoly store has increased its service of guiding consumers in their choice of alcohol, the statistics of alcohol consumption per capita have declined. Also, the statistics show a tendency for people to consume less strong liquor and spirits and more low-alcohol percentage averages, which overall is considered a healthier consumption pattern for society.

Liberation Continues

In recent years, the Faroe Islands have seen a significant expansion of new alcohol products. This happened after the law on alcohol from 1992 was made less restrictive in 2011, making it legal to produce spirits with an alcohol limit of up to 60% alcohol. Before this change, the law prohibited producing anything above 5,8 %, which is why many traditional Faroese beers have that exact strength. Another change made with the 2011 changes was the legalisation of using cans instead of bottles. Before these changes, producers were prohibited from using anything but bottles, making production and recycling more expensive.

However, the changes in the revised Alcohol Act did not come by themselves. Restaurants, the hospitality industry, and, of course, breweries strongly advocated for less restricted regulation. The restaurants and hotels wanted to be able to serve more potent liquor. At the same time, the breweries pointed out the hypocrisy when it was illegal to brew or distil similar products to what was imported and sold in Rúsan. But, at that time, the Faroese politicians did not seem to bother making changes to the legislation. But that all changed in 2008 when DISM, the first "Faroese distillery," was established.

The Distillery that Exemplified the Absurdities

With founders closely tied with the whisky and beer enthusiast societies, the brewery DISM was founded with a vision of making local Faroese spirits. However, they could not set up a brewery on the islands because it was illegal then.

DISM was one of those advocating for new alcohol legislation. They pointed out the strange contradiction that you could import spirits from all over the world while distilling locally was prohibited. Although they tried to apply for special approval, it could not be done. Therefore, they decided to take matters into their own hands and highlight the absurdities of the rules in such a way that it became clear to everyone.

Soon, it was announced that they were working on making purely Faroese snaps, the *Lívsins Vatn* akvavit, and that they had already begun setting up production in Iceland and Denmark. They started exporting fresh Faroese water to Denmark and Iceland, distilled their spirits there, and then imported them back to the Faroes. In that way, one might consider DISM an authentic Faroese distillery, though they have never had their products made there.

It worked as planned. The exporting of fresh water to distil, only to import it again as alcohol, made people wonder about the law. Soon, a heated debate started on softening the restrictive Alcohol Act from 1992. Here, it became clear that DISM played a massive role in pushing for a revision.

Chapter Ten

Faroese Currencies

LEGO-Money or a Predecessor to Cryptocurrency?

The currency of the Faroe Islands is the Danish krone, which closely follows the Euro. Even though Faroese paper money could make one believe that the money is Faroese, it has a distinct design and gets printed by the Faroese banks. However, this is not true since its currency is entirely Danish, and the coins used are Danish.

During World War II, the Danish money applicable on the islands was made distinct by being stamped with red ink saying: *"Kun gyldig paa Færøerne. Færø Amt, Juni 1940,"* translated *"Only valid on the Faroe Islands. Faroe County, June 1940."* By stamping the paper money, the Faroes could separate their currency from that of Denmark, which Germany occupied then. Like with paper money, coins were also drilled into separating the coins. The stamped paper money and drilled coins were the only valid currency on the islands, and they could not be used in Denmark or vice versa.

Privately owned currencies

Like crypto valuta today, there used to be currencies that were alternative to the currency that was backed by the state. These were privately owned by companies who, in the years 1929 to 1933, when the Faroe Islands were in a deep financial crisis, tried to solve the problem of simply having too few coins fluctuating in the society, which caused enormous problems for the companies when they had to pay their workers. To solve this problem, the companies started with a booking system where the workers had to register their working hours, and a given number of hours resulted in vouchers that could only be used in stores owned by the company they worked for.

At that time, the companies owned the fishing vessels, fish factories, and drugstores, making the workers entirely dependent on them for their income and everyday spending.

The newly implemented booking system quickly resulted in the workers registering too many working hours compared to how much they had worked. The companies then tried another system where workers and employers registered daily hours. When these numbers didn't add up, it caused immense dissatisfaction and many quarrels between employers and employees.

Clergyman Samuel Peter Petersen in Fuglafjørður then got the idea of making his own set of coins to pay his workers, which he had made in a factory in Bilbao, Spain, that specialised in making casino tokens. The authorities did not recognise the coins, which could only be used at his personal store. These coins solved the problems the booking system couldn't, and already a year later, in 1930, clergyman Jógvan Fredrik Kjølbro from Klaksvík had copied S. P. Petersen's idea for his own company J. F. Kjølbro.

Coins by Kjølbro. Photo by Rúni í Múla.

Even though the Danish state did not recognise the coins, people grew confident in their actual value since they could be used for goods in stores. Seeing that trust had been placed in these currencies, people started trading the different coins, which increased the demand for the coins—so much so that official Danish krones often were traded because they had no higher value in practice.

The private currencies quickly ended when, in 1933, Danish authorities banned them. They confiscated all the coins from both companies by gathering them together and throwing them into the sea.

Coins by J. F. Kjølbro, Klaksvík (1930 - 1933).

- 10 øre

- 25 øre

- 50 øre

- 1 krone

- 2 krone

- 5 krone

- 10 krone

The coins had a round shape and varied in size.

Coins by S. P. Petersens Eftf, Fuglafjørður (1929 - 1933).

- 5 øre

- 10 øre

- 25 øre

- 1 krone

- 2 krone

- 5 krone

The coins were made of brass and varied in shape and size, with some containing extensive writing and some small. Some had the writing EPTF and some EFTF.

Chapter Eleven

Vehicles and Vessels

Barrel Vehicles and Mountain-built Catamarans

Although the Faroe Islands have nearly no trees, an old boat-building tradition goes far back to the Viking age. The boats that have been built have been made from driftwood, imported wood, and wood that washed ashore from shipwrecks.

It is said that the first Faroese ship, Royndin Fríða, was built in Vágur in the early 1800s. This ship was built from recycled wood from an English cargo vessel abandoned in the Faroes because of its poor condition. The Faroese national hero, Nólsoyar Páll, bought the wreckage at an auction in Tórshavn, and with it, he built Royndin Fríða with help from four other men.

In newer times, from around 1900 to the millennium, many steel ships have been built in the two leading shipyards, Tórshavn Shipyard and Skála Shipyard. In the 1960s especially, many ships were built in Skála, which grew rapidly as a village during those years. Today, the shipyard's main work is doing repairs, although some boats are still being built.

The Traditional Faroese Boat

The traditional Faroese boat is derived from the Norn clinker boat. Still, through the ages, the Faroese boat has been adapted to Faroese needs which have been fisheries, whale hunting and transporting goods and livestock between the islands. Boatbuilding is a tradition passed down through the generations where the elder boat builders have taught the younger ones and have never been part of any formalised education.

Even though the Faroese boat is still being built for the traditional Faroese rowing sport, the demand for such boats is deficient. Modern fibreglass boats are better suited for harsh weather conditions and are geared with modern equipment. Building such boats takes hundreds of hours and is therefore of very high-end quality and expensive. This has caused a decline in new boats being built. Additionally, it must be said that only ten boat builders who know the old building tradition are left. With the lack of apprentices to carry on with this tradition, the Faroese boat must be considered to be highly threatened.

In a report from 2012, the Ministry of Culture estimated that the boat-building tradition might be lost in about 20 years if the younger generation doesn't take up this tradition. But, there might still be hope because recently, there have been a handful of young men who have started as apprentices for boat building and also, on the 14th of December 2021, the traditional Faroese boat became part of the UNESCO World Heritage List together with the conventional clinker boats from the other Nordic countries.

Boatbuilding in a Mountain Village

KJ Hydraulik was founded in 1978 as a small mechanical workshop in Fuglafjørður, focusing on hydraulic systems. It has since expanded into the largest mechanical workshop on the Faroe Islands, specialising in hydraulics and the salmon industry.

Today, it has three central departments: the Administrative, Sales, and Technical departments, with the third mentioned having four subdivisions: the Mechanical shop, the Forklift division, the Entrepreneur division, and the Automatic division.

In the late 80s, the workshop moved to the mountain village of Kambsdalur, a satellite village from Fuglafjørður. In this mountain village, some 135 meters above sea level, KJ Hydraulik has a boatbuilding shop that produces high-quality catamarans designed for salmon farming, which the firm exports to salmon farmers worldwide.

Because the catamarans are built on a mountain, it is not without strains when these boats get floated. When they are ready, they are transported by large trailers from Kambsdalur to the neighbouring town of Fuglafjørður. When this happens, the roads get closed, and sometimes, light posts have to be removed to make space for transporting the larger models through the town and to the dock. The challenges with transport have led the company to buy an old wharf in Fuglafjørður Harbour, where the largest barges are built today.

The Danga

It is said that when Faroese fishermen first came to England to buy the wooden schooners, which made it possible for them to go far out to sea to their fisheries, they bought vessels, which they called Danga. Danga is a common Faroese word today, and the meaning of this word is something like 'an old wooden, beaten-up ship.'

The vessels they bought were all labelled with signs saying 'Danger,' and because the Faroese were so bad at English, they mistook these signs for being a type of vessel instead of a ship in poor shape.

This story has often been told as a joke, but in Dr Tórður Jóansson's doctorate thesis about English loanwords in Faroese, he argues that the story is true. Linguists and historians tend to agree with Dr Jóansson even though the account has many variations.

The "Dream Car"

In the 1950s, a Norwegian man called Almar Nordhaug built a car that he named the Dream Car (Later, in Norway, the Aeroplane). With help from colleagues, Nordhaug had the car built in a barrel factory in Tórshavn, and when it was finished, its futuristic design was of much amusement for the locals when it was seen driving in the streets of Tórshavn and the Faroe Islands in general.

The car was based on the Vauxhall Cresta chassis, drivetrain, and engine, and its design took great inspiration from the 1954 Ford concept car called the FX-Atmos. Its handmade body and roof, taken from an aeroplane, made it look like something from a 1950s sci-fi sitcom. It also had loudspeakers and a cassette player, which had never been seen before, adding to the car's innovative and futuristic feel.

Nordhaug drove around in his homemade vehicle for a while, but eventually, he moved back to Norway in 1957 and brought the car with him.

The Dream Car, driven by Nordhaug. Photo by unknown.

He also drove the car there for some years, but it was in bad condition and was set for sale in the early 1960s. Nils Petter Weiberg Aurdal bought it at a used car dealership, restored it, and then sold it again to a furniture company in Oslo called Grefa, which used it as a display car.

Nobody knows what became of the car. There are contradicting rumours: some say the vehicle was destroyed some years ago, while others still believe it is kept safe although hidden away.

Faroese Custom cars

One of the most famous custom carmakers is Sofus Hansen in Tórshavn. Throughout his life, he has rebuilt many different car models; his rebuilds are not regular customisations, but with his keen eye for detail and high skills as a modifier, his rebuilds are pure design transformations.

In his home garage, he has his workshop, where his rebuilds have all been made. In the early years, he kept his work modest, mixing a Volkswagen Beetle with a Rolls Royce and rebuilding a Chevrolet Stingray into something resembling the 1989 Batmobile. But he has taken his building to a new level in recent years.

One of his most famous rebuilds was a 1991 Porsche 928 S4. For this build, he won a prize in Sweden for the best custom-built car and made headlines in various car magazines.

Chapter Twelve

Cinematography and Movies

And the Death of James Bond

In recent years, the Faroe Islands have become an increasingly popular scenery for cinematics in the film industry. Even though it was rumoured to be scheduled as one of the filming locations for Peter Jackson's The Lord of the Rings trilogy, this rumour has never been confirmed even though it is easy to imagine with the beautiful scenery and unspoiled nature. But scenes from the Faroes have since been used for films such as *Submergence* (2017) starring Alicia Vikander and James McAvoy and series such as *Trom* (2022) starring Ulrik Thomsen and Faroese actor Olaf Johannesen. The islet of Tindhólmur has also been used in the series *His Dark Materials* (2019) and serves as the island where the witches live, and in the new Disney production of *Peter Pan & Wendy* (2023), scenes have also been used in some of the islands, cliffs and sea stacks. The most extensive film set that has ever been to the Faroe Islands is, without question, the *James Bond* movie, *No Time to Die*, which hit the cinema in 2021.

No Time to Die

The movie *No Time to Die* (2021) is Daniel Craig's last movie as James Bond. This is evident at the movie's end when Bond dies from a large missile strike after realising that he was infected by nanobots which makes him unable to touch his daughter Mathilde or his beloved Madeliene, played by actress Léa Seydoux.

Like the other Bond films, No Time to Die has an extensive range of filming locations, one of them being on the Faroe Islands, which is the location that serves as the death place of 007.

In the movie, the villain's island is supposed to be a Japanese island, but its filming location is actually in a place called Kallur which is on the northernmost part of the island of Kallsoy.

On the place where Agent 007 died now resides a tombstone which says the following:

IN MEMORY OF

JAMES BOND 1962 - 2021

THE PROPER FUNCTION OF MAN IS TO LIVE, NOT EXIST.

The mock tombstone was erected on March 21, 2022, by the farmer of Trøllanes, Jóhannus Kallsgarð, who owns the land where the scenes were shot and is credited in the movie's end credits as "King of Kallsoy."

James Bond's Mock Tombstone. Photo by Georgi Kalaydzhiev on Unsplash.

The quote on the tombstone is the words that M, played by actor Ralph Fiennies, reads at Bond's funeral in the end scene of the movie *No Time to Die* from 2021. The full quote is ascribed initially to the American author Jack London and goes as follows:

"The proper function of man is to live, not to exist. I shall not spend my days in trying to prolong them. I shall use my time."

Ian Flemming later used it to describe James Bond in the novel *You Only Live Twice* (1964), where the world at one point thinks that Bond has died. The quote is the end part of Jack London's original writing, which goes as follows:

"I would rather be ashes than dust! I would rather that my spark should burn out in a brilliant blaze than it should be stifled by dry-rot. I would rather be a superb meteor, every atom of me in magnificent glow, than a sleepy and permanent planet. The proper function of man is to live, not to exist. I shall not waste my days in trying to prolong them. I shall use my time."

Skyfall

Even though *No Time to Die* was the first time the James Bond franchise was in the Faroe Islands, there's reason to believe that the James Bond movies have had influence deriving from the Faroes.

In his lifetime, Ian Flemming wrote only 14 novels and nine short stories about the James Bond character. Still, there have been 25 movie instalments on the big screen.

When Flemming died on the 12th of August 1964, some of his short stories, which are included in the nine mentioned stories, were published posthumously. After his death, other authors continued writing about Agent 007. Some of these post publications have been the novels behind movies such as *Licence to Kill* (1989), but even though many more James Bond titles are available, the movie *Skyfall* (2012) was not among these titles.

Instead, this movie takes great inspiration from another spy book - one from a book series about a character who has influenced James Bond before in the film *Moonraker* from 1979.

There are good reasons to believe that the storyline of *Skyfall* was highly inspired by John Buckham's 1939 novel *The Island of Sheep*. This idea was discussed in a 2019 Faroese article, which analysed and compared the storyline of the book and the film. The article concludes that *Skyfall* is highly inspired by the book, which was supported by comparable coincidences in both stories, such as the story itself, place names, events and so on. The fact that John Buckham's books have inspired Ian Fleming further substantiates this point of view, in addition to the fact that the few original James Bond titles that have still not been used in the film series are limited. Therefore, this is also a good solution for a film company that intends to produce more James Bond films.

One of the lines from the article claims that: '[...] *he* (James Bond) *was here before we knew it.*'

Chapter Thirteen

Public Service and Bingo

The Public Radio and Television Broadcasting Service

The National Public Service radio and television broadcaster, Kringvarp Føroya (KVF), is funded through demanded pay for anyone who has turned 18 years old. Even though the payment is demanded, it has been kept separate from the tax system securing funding without political interference.

Kringvarp Føroya was originally two different broadcasting services. The radio, Útvarp Føroya, was founded in 1957 and the television, Sjónvarp Føroya, in 1984. In 2005 these two public broadcasting services merged into one broadcasting station, which is part of the public service, comparable to BBC, but smaller.

As a public service, the broadcasting station is inclined to produce and broadcast a wide range of content, some of which have been to great amusement among the public.

Gekkurin - a Cultural Treasure of playing Bingo

Every Friday at 8 pm, KVF has a bingo programme where people can play along in their homes via television. The programme is called Gekkur and is one of the national broadcaster's primary incomes. It has been running for more than 25 years (since February 1997) and is funded by sponsorship and by people who buy their bingo plates each week.

In this bingo programme, random numbers are shown on the television screen, and from home, people match these numbers with their bingo plates. In the first three games, players must get a row on one of the plates and then call to live television to select a letter. Behind these letters, the winners can choose between different gift vouchers. In the game's fourth round, players must get a full plate and then call the television programme. One of the lucky winners then gets to turn the Gekkur wheel of fortune, where they can win a relatively large sum of money.

The programme has shown to be so popular that it is a standard part of everyday conversation and small talk where the question often is asked: *Are you going to play Gekkur tonight?*

Due to its popularity, the programme sometimes has its own house band, which plays background music while the game of bingo is ongoing. The band is called Konfekt, and its band members are some of the most experienced and best-known musicians from the Faroe Islands who are known to have worked with artists such as Eivør and Teitur, etc.

The band has proven so popular that it attended the annual G! Festival in 2016 and the yearly Summarfestivalur in 2011, the two largest competing annual music festivals in the Faroe Islands.

The Weather Forecast Broadcasting

Each day, the weather forecast is broadcast as part of the news program on radio and television. The weather forecast has been part of radio and television stations since the beginning. This stems from when the Faroe Islands only had Norwegian radio. To this day, when people ask about the weather, they ask: *Hvat sigur norðmaðurin?* - What does the Norwegian guy say?

The old Faroese people used to be very interested in the weather conditions. When the radio first came to the Faroese and the weather broadcast reported lousy weather, the locals blamed the weathercast hosts.

The Announcement of Deaths and Funerals

Each day at three o'clock, the names of every person diseased are read on the radio after the three o'clock news and can also be read on the website KVF. fo. The announcement covers the name, birth name, nickname, age, where they come from and where they lived. This includes residents living on the Faroes and people residing abroad. Here the funeral is also announced, and people can pay their respects by donating money to charity organisations or family members to cover the funeral costs, etc.

Sometimes, when a person of particular interest to the public is diseased, and reporters need a news story, they make a profile depicting the person's life, importance, contribution to society, etc.

Christmas Greetings from Abroad

Every Christmas, the radio broadcasts Christmas greetings from Faroese people who live, study, or work abroad. This old tradition is still followed, although the distances today are different from when it initially came into effect.

Christmas greetings are trendy amongst the locals; for many, they are an integrated part of their annual Christmas traditions.

Some of these greetings are often cited where people make fun of the pronunciation of people who have lived abroad for a long time or children who haven't quite learned Faroese properly.

Chapter Fourteen

World Records

And Wild Achievements

Although the Faroe Islands is a small country with only approximately 55,000 inhabitants, the Faroese people have made many remarkable and outstanding achievements, both in historical and modern times.

In this chapter, I will try to introduce a selection of these impressive achievements that people have made throughout the years, some of which can seem unbelievable. These are stories about Nobel Prize winners, the world's oldest siblings, a Faroese explorer who was one of the first Europeans ever to travel to Siberia, explorers of the sea, etc.

The Nobel Prize in Medicine and Physiology

Niels Ryberg Finsen (b. 1860 - d. 1904) was a Faroese physician and scientist of Icelandic descent who, since 1903, was the only Faroese person ever to receive a Nobel Prize. However, William Heinesen was nominated for the Prize in Literature in the late 1970s, which he rejected.

Niels Ryberg Finsen. Unknown Photographer.

Finsen was born and raised in Tór-shavn, where he also started in school. But at an early age, he was sent to a boarding school in Her-lufsholm in Denmark, where his old-er brother was also studying. He was considered unsuited as a student be-cause of his poor presentation and low grades. Therefore, he was sent to his father's old school in Iceland, where he continued his studies. In 1876, at 21, he graduated in Iceland, but at his graduation, he was number 11 of 15 students.

In 1882, he moved to Copenhagen to study medicine. This time, however, he would show much more talent than he had earlier. After graduation, he became increasingly involved in teaching at the University of Copenhagen. Eventually, in 1898, he received his professorship but was, at that point, mainly focusing on his scientific research within the field of light therapy.

In 1903 he was awarded a Nobel Prize in Medicine and Physiology for his contribution to treating skin diseases using light radiation. He was the first person from the Faroes to be awarded the Nobel Prize and the first person in Scandinavia to get the prize.

Because of this, the Faroe Islands became the country in the world with the most Nobel Prize winners per capita, and to this day, it still is.

Sigert, the Faroese Explorer

At the age of 20, in 1889, a young Faroese man from Kirkjubø, Sigert Patursson, left his home country to travel the world on a journey that eventually would have him spend many years in western Siberia.

He first came to Scotland, then Denmark and Sweden. In January 1990, he set off for Siberia, an unexplored territory for most of Europe at that time. Life in Siberia was unknown, and there were no roads or railways, so he had to walk and use sledges on his journey.

When he arrived, he spent six years with the original inhabitants of Siberia. From his experience there, he wrote a twelve-bound book from 1900 to 1901, which sold well and sparked people's curiosity in Europe. After travelling in Siberia, he was invited to give speeches and give lectures across Europe. Journalists took great interest in him everywhere he went and published many articles in the respective countries.

He continued his travels by holding lectures and visiting Norway, Finland, Russia, and Sweden again. In Sweden and Norway, where he wrote his book, he also published many articles about his travels, which were very well received.

Sigert Patursson Holding a Globe and a Faroese Flag. Photo by Gustav Borgen, Norsk Folkemuseum.

However, the explorations were not the only reason people took an interest in him. He was always very well dressed and had political ideas that many thought radical. He dreamt of a joint world order where every nation would unite. He wrote and published articles on the topic and had ideas about psychology, pedagogics, and esthetics, which he also wrote about.

Later, in 1907, he travelled to Mongolia, Korea, the Middle East, France, Poland, Egypt, and many other countries, which was unusual for any citizen then. Still, for a Faroese person, it was unheard of.

He took his idea of a joint world seriously, and in his later writings, he would always sign them 'Sigert Patursson the First of the World.'

The Olsen Siblings

In The Guinness Book of World Records 2017, the Olsen siblings from Rituvík on Eysturoy had the highest combined age of twelve living siblings.

To document and prove this record, the twelve siblings, seven brothers and five sisters, had to gather information about themselves, which they had relatives and government officials to help them with. This proved challenging because many of them had never received a birth certificate or passport, making the process long and sturdy.

On August 14, 2014, it was confirmed that they had reached the high age of *1.025 years and 41 days* combined.

- Magnus Salomon "Maggi" (b. the 30th of October 1920)

- Vensil (b. 8th of October 1921)

- Sára Malena (b. the 20th of February 1923)

- Marin Fredrikka (b. 18th of August 1924)

- Arnholt Sofus (b. the 28th of September 1925)

- Carl Sivar (b. the 25th of January 1928)

- Elly (b. the 14th of February 1930)

- Jaspur (b. the 24th of July 1932)

- Harry (the 3rd of September 1933)

- Mary Elina (b. the 8th of December 1934)

- Amy (b. the 6th of September 1936)

- Arni Kartni (b. the 30th of June 1938)

On the 9th of July 2017, Maggie, the oldest brother, sadly passed away, making their final age count *1.059 years, eight months, and 22 days*. This last count has, however, not been confirmed by Guinness.

On December 15, 2020, Guinness World Records announced that the D'Cruz family from Pakistan had beaten the record set by the Olsen siblings. Their record was set at *1.042 years and 315 days*, making their combined age some *44 years younger than the final age count for the Olsens*. However, according to the Guinness Book of Records, the D'Cruz family still holds the official record.

Tróndur Patursson

Tróndur Patursson (b. 1944) is one of the most famous artists from the Faroe Islands. He has held art exhibitions worldwide and is a recognised name in fine art paintings.

But when Tróndur was young, he was also a seafarer and a prolific adventurer who traveled on the world's seven seas.

Inspired by the legend of St. Brendan, who is said to be the first Irish monk to settle on the Faroe Islands and who is said to have arrived by skin boat and travelled as far as the Americas, Tróndur decided to see whether it was possible to do such a voyage using such a boat.

In 1976, Tróndur and Tim Simerin decided to make the same voyage as St. Brendan. With a boat built in the same fashion as leather boats from around the year 600, they sailed from the Faroe Islands to Iceland and then to Newfoundland. The boat was named Brandan after the Irish monk.

Rowed Across the Atlantic Ocean

In 2018, three Faroese men and a man from New Zealand set a new world record for rowing the furthest distance ever recorded. The men, Jákup Jacobsen, Jógvan Clementsen, Niclas Olsen, and Isaac Giesen (NZ), left port in Portugal on February 10. 74 days later, they landed in Cuba on May 12 after rowing 8.000 kilometres in one go.

Livar Nysted

Livar Nysted (b. 1970) is a Faroese painter and athlete. Although he might be better known for his paintings, he has set several records in rowing. He started indoor rowing at 27 but eventually started rowing out on the fjords.

In 2013, he and two other men, Maxime Chaya from Libanon and Stuart Kershaw from England, crossed the Indian Ocean by rowing. When they finished their trip, they set the record for being the fastest to have rowed across the Indian Ocean and having the smallest crew cross the Indian Ocean by rowing.

Nysted has made several trips across oceans and is the first to row across two of the world's seven seas in the same year.

The World's First Underwater Roundabout

In 2020, the sub-sea tunnel Eysturoyartunnilin opened, connecting the two sides of the Skálafjørður fjord in Eysturoy with Tórshavn. This sub-sea tunnel is the third of its kind in the Faroe Islands and the second time Eysturoy and Streymoy have been connected.

Unlike the two previous subsea tunnels, this one has three entrances and a roundabout which connects the three tunnel entrances. In the world, tunnels have been built before that contain a roundabout, but according to the World Record Academy, this was the first time a roundabout has ever been built in a subsea tunnel.

The tunnel is generally received as a groundbreaking investment in the Faroese infrastructure, making a better connection between the two largest and most populated areas in the Faroes. However, people have been critiquing the high costs of the toll road, which is, however, becoming cheaper as the years pass and the government's debt of building the tunnel is being paid off.

To honour this investment in the infrastructure and to celebrate the fact that this tunnel is the first of its kind with a roundabout, the roundabout is decorated by artist Tróndur Patursson. The art piece is the silhouettes of people dancing the Faroese chain dance. Also, as an added feature, the prominent musician Jens L. Thomsen, best known for the electronic band Orka, has made a musical piece, which one can tune in on using the car radio, made by mixing the sounds of the tunnel. This track can be heard on the radio channel **FM 97,0**.

Dollin and the Exposure of The Congo Atrocities During the Belgian Rule

Ludvig Daniel Jacob Danielsen (b. 1871 – d. 1916), nicknamed Dollin, was a Faroese missionary who became well-known for exposing the Force Publique's exploitation of natives during King Leopold II of Belgium's sole ownership of the Congo Free State.

When he was 18, Dollin moved to Scotland, where he trained to become a maritime engineer. During his time there, he was introduced to the Christian Brethren movement, and after having had a religious awakening, he became an active member of the Seamen's Movement in Glasgow. The movement in Glasgow soon connected him with missionaries in Africa, which appealed to Dollin's curiosity.

In 1900, Dollin saw a job opening as an engineer on a missionary boat that sailed on the Congo River. He felt adventurous and applied for the job, and in 1901, he started working there as they sailed to and from the Bonginda district. Although his primary task was to take care of the boat engines, he felt he had to use his missionary convictions to participate in missionary work, which he was allowed to and would do occasionally. In addition, he also had a great fascination for photography and always had his camera with him, where he documented the time on board the boat.

Having worked on board for two years, he and the other crew members had been in close contact with the people of the Congo, which at times was marked by conflict. In 1903, an employee accused Dollin of torturing a local man. This accusation was taken very seriously, and although Dollin was acquitted of the charges, this marked the end of his time on the boat. On his return journey, he met the English consul, Roger Casement, who was investigating accusations against the Force Publique concerning brutalities suffered by the Congolese.

To do his job, Caseman needed a machinist to take care of the boat he needed to cross the Congo River, and he asked Dollin if he was willing to help, which he was. They travelled together, with Caseman reporting what he saw while Dollin cared for the machinery. During this time, Dollin kept to his photography hobby, documenting their journey and everything happening there using pictures.

Roger Caseman completed his report, which showed a very violent and brutal repression of the Congolese people, which substantiated the accusations levelled against Belgian rule. Here, it became clear that Force Publique used cutting off hands as one of the punishment methods, which Dollin substantiated with his pictures.

When Caseman reported to England, it created a sensation and made headlines worldwide. But in his address to the English Government, he said that all the work could not have been accomplished without the assistance he had received from Dollin.

Dollin was offered a large reward for his part of the work but would not accept it. Instead, he said that all rewards should be given to the people of the Congo, which England respected.

Dollin subsequently had exhibitions with pictures in England and the Faroe Islands, showcasing the atrocities the Congolese people had suffered.

Chapter Fifteen

Fun Facts

Language

- The Faroe Islands means "Sheep Islands."

- The Faroese language, widely spoken by everyone on the islands, is most closely related to Icelandic and the Old Norse language, which does not exist today.

- The Faroese alphabet contains eight letters that are not found in English, which are Á, Í, Ó, Ú, Ý, Æ, Ø and Ð, plus an additional three combined letters, which, in the Faroese alphabet, are perceived as being letters in and of themselves; Ei, Ey, and Oy.

- The alphabet does not include the letters C, Q, X and Z.

- There are three official languages: Faroese, Danish and Faroese sign language.

- Since June 2017, Faroese sign language has been formally recognised as an official language. However, no school offers lectures in Faroese sign language.

- English is taught at school by fourth grade and is spoken by most of the population.

- The word *Sjeikur* is Faroese for boyfriend. It derives from Rodolph Valentino's movie *The Sheik* from 1920, which became so popular that the word Sheik became synonymous with the word boyfriend. Today, "sjeikur" is the most used word for boyfriend.

- In Faroese, the word *danga* is like a beaten-up rotten ship. The word is said to derive from when Faroese fishermen first came to England to buy used schooners for the Faroese fishing fleet. Since they didn't know English then, they bought vessels with signs reading "danger" on them.

- In Faroese, there are 37 words for fog and 140 words for rain.

- In the Faculty of Faroese Language and Literature at the University of the Faroe Islands, there is a safe that contains every word in the Faroese language. These words were collected around the islands around the same time as the university was established. Ever since, new words have been added after being accepted by the Faroese Language Council.

- The most common word for being dull is *býttur*. Directly translated, it means "being switched," which stems from the old superstitious belief of the hidden people, who were believed to be a kind of elves who lived in a parallel society inaccessible by people. It was believed that dull people had been switched as infants with the children of the hidden people. This same belief can also be found in Icelandic superstition.

- In Danish, it is often stated that other languages do not have a word for the Danish word *hygge*. This is false because this word also exists in Faroese and is called *hugni*.

- In Danish, the word *tjald* is a common slang for cannabis. The word stems from the 1970s when the Faroese passenger ship Tjaldrið used to sail between Denmark and the Faroes. At that time, cannabis was smuggled and could be bought at the same dock, hense the word *tjald*.

- In 2024 the Faroese language was included in Google Translate.

- Many words in English have a Norse origin (the language of the Vikings), which highly resembles modern Faroese and modern Icelandic. Such words include *father, mother, husband, knife, crook, loan, egg, steak, freckle, window, ill, die, rotten, skill,* and many others, including pronounces such as *they* and *their*.

Culture

- The national bird is not the puffin. It is the oystercatcher.

- It is often said that the Faroe Islands have 70.000 sheep. According to the Agricultural Agency, Búnaðarstovan, and the Environment Agency, Umhvørvisstovan, this number is just an estimation because there has never been an actual sheep counting. The estimation is based on how many sheep are allowed on all the different land properties around the islands and does not consider the young sheep. How many sheep there are is unknown.

- In September 1990, the Faroese football team won their first tournament game versus Austria, resulting in a great Faroese celebration.

- The island of Koltur is the only national park in the country. It became a national park in 2018 and will serve as a nature reserve and research station. The plan is to remove all grazing animals so that researchers can investigate the flora in its natural habitat without animal interference.

- In 2016, National Geographic Traveler elected the Faroe Islands as the most appealing island destination from a selected list of archipelagos.

- In 2021, the Faroe Islands were chosen as 1 of the 30 best places to travel by Lonely Planet.

- Since December 14th 2021, the traditional Faroese clinker boat has been included in the UNESCO List of Intangible Cultural Heritage of Humanity.

- Ólavsøka is held annually on the 28th and 29th of July and is often seen as the national holiday. However, the Faroe Islands do not technically have a national holiday.

- Although Ólavsøka is not technically a Faroese national day, in March 2016, the Danish government decided to make Ólavsøka a Danish flag-flying day, even though the Faroese flag day is on March 25th. The decision to choose Ólavsøka over the official flag day in the Faroe Islands caused great surprise among several Danish and Faroese politicians. Still, the decision was made anyway, and Denmark made Ólavsøka an official flag day in Denmark.

- On July 29th 2016 all Danish institutions were obligated to celebrate the Faroe Islands by raising the Faroese flag for the first time. It turned out to be the wrong flag that was raised on the flagpoles – the colours were right but had been switched around. In 2018, the correct flag was raised, but this was on the wrong day, June 29th. This reoccured on the same day in 2020 and 2021.

- Although *Tú Alfagra Land Mítt* (Thou Fairest Land of Mine) is best known as the national anthem, it technically isn't, as it is not stated in any legislation. In some places, this song is not recognised as the national anthem; instead, two other songs are competing; one is called *Boðar Tú Til Allar Tjóðir* (When Thou Send Word to all Nations), and the other is *Eg Oyggjar Veit* (I Know Some Islands).

- The Faroese chain dance was common in Europe in the Middle Ages, but this tradition has vanished in all other European countries. The chain dance is still alive in the Faroes and is being danced to a chanting called kvæði.

- Gunnar Nielsen, a defender for Motherwell in Scotland, is the only footballer from the island to have participated in the Premier League.

- Faroese superstition says many mythical beings live in the mountains and at sea. These creatures include giants, trolls, kelpies, pixies, selkies, mermaids and mermen, sea ghosts, regular ghosts, and hidden people, who are elfish people living in a parallel society.

- In Skopun, there is the world's second-largest mailbox. According to the Guinness Book of World Records, it was the world's most oversized mailbox when it was built.

- The 1884 novella *Manor* by the famous German author and LGBT activist Karl Heinrich Ulrichs introduced the vampire for the first time in the Faroe Islands. This is 13 years prior to Bram Stoker's Dracula.

- Actor James McAvoy (b. 1979) is the first internationally recognised actor to have played in two different movie sets set in the Faroe Islands: the movie *Submergence* (2017) and the series *His Dark Materials* (2019 - 2022).

- The largest movie set ever filmed in the Faroe Islands is the James Bond movie *No Time to Die* (2021).

- Disney's *Peter Pan & Wendy* (2023) was the second largest movie.

- In 2023, Danish astronaut Anders Mogensen was sent to the International Space Station, and with him, he brought the Danish, Greenlandic, and Faroese flags.

- In addition to the flags, Anders Mogensen also brought a woollen tie with him that used to belong to the prominent Faroese author and artist William Heinesen.

History

- Archaeological excavations have shown that people lived on the islands in the year 300, although nothing is known of those people.

- Irish monks were the first people known to have settled on the Faroe Islands. This is supported by archaeological excavations, document analysis from British documents, and placenames, which indicate an Irish presence. Examples of placenames are Vestmanna, meaning West Men, and Saksun, meaning Saxon, and Mykines, which combines the Celtic words Muk and Innis, which translates into Colt Isle.

- Norwegian Vikings first arrived around the year 800.

- The first Norse settlement is believed to be in the village of Funningur in Eysturoy.

- Around the Viking settlement, Frisians also arrived in Suðuroy. They lived in a parallel society and kept to themselves on the southern part of the southernmost island. When the Black Plague struck the Faroes, it claimed the lives of the majority of the Frisian colony. According to legend, only two survived and are said to have married other Faroese people.

• The Faroese parliament, Løgtingið, is among the oldest parliaments in the world. It was first used in 825.

• Sverrir Sigurðsson, King of Norway (b. 1177 - d. 1202), was born and raised in Kirkjubø.

• The Black Plague struck in 1349, killing one-third of the population.

• The farmhouse in Kirkjubø is one of the oldest wooden houses in the world, which is still in use. Its oldest parts were built around the year 1350.

• From 1500 to 1700, pirate invasions of the Faroe Islands were severe. The pirates were primarily from France and Turkey.

• Jonas Bronck (b. 1600 – d. 1643), whom the Bronx River and the Bronx in New York City are named after, is believed to have emigrated from Denmark to the United States of America. Some believe him to be of Swedish descent, while others believe him to be Faroese. Nonetheless, in Tórshavn, there's a street named Jónas Broncks Gøta after him.

• The potato was first mentioned in writing in Vestmanna in 1686, 51 years before Denmark and 64 years before Norway.

- In the early 1800s, Napoleon Bonaparte was said to have visited the islands on his journey in the North Atlantic. This has not been confirmed. However, the French fleet sailed the North Atlantic during this time, and Napoleon Bonaparte took part in that voyage.

- The Faroe Islands were part of Norway until 1814 when Denmark lost Norway to Sweden in the Tready of Kiel which ended the Napoleonic Wars. Up until that point, Iceland and Greenland were part of Norway too, and became part of Denmark as well. Historians debate whether this happened by an administrative mistake in Norway or if the islands were simply forgotten during the political negotiations.

- Niels Ryberg Finsen (b. 1860 - d. 1904) was a Faroese doctor who received the Nobel Prize in 1903 for his medical contribution to treating diseases with concentrated light radiation, especially lupus vulgaris (tuberculosis on the skin).

- The Faroe Islands has the world's most Nobel Prize winners per capita.

- Runic stones have been found nationwide, the most famous being the Fámjin Stone, the Kirkjubø Stone, and the Sandavágur Stone. These are the three most significant ones, though another stone is believed to hold significance: the Froðba Stone. It was found in the mid-1800s and is currently kept in the National Museum in Denmark. Runes have also been carved into wood and kept in the National Museum in Tórshavn.

- In the hymn book of the Faroese church, there is a hymn attributed to Tróndur í Gøtu (Thrand of Gata), who is said to have been the greatest chieftain of the Faroe Islands according to the Saga of the Faroe Islanders. However, there is no evidence to support his authorship. In fact, it appears to be a case of historical manipulation based on the saga, which is the only written record of the Faroe Islands from that era.

- During World War II, Britain occupied the Faroe Islands. The islands were flooded with British soldiers, and at one point, approximately 8.000 British soldiers were staying there.

- During the war, 205 Faroese fishermen lost their lives at sea. This is the highest death rate per capita during the war.

- In 1992, the Faroe Islands experienced a severe economic depression. Over 10% of the country's population left, and 25% of those who remained were unemployed.

Politics

- Although Denmark is part of the European Union, the Faroe Islands are not.

- Because the islands are not part of the European Union, all trades with the EU are handled by bilateral agreements.

- Women had their first vote in 1906 and voted for legislation which banned the use of alcohol.

- Although they had voted in 1906, women got the official right to vote in 1916, one year later than Denmark and 13 years before women in the United Kingdom.

- In 1946, the Faroe Islands voted for independence from Denmark. The vote was dismissed because the results were not deemed convincing.

- The abortion law from 1956 strictly prohibits abortions. Whether abortion should be legalised is an ongoing debate that has divided the two opposing sides.

- In 1988, FIFA was the first international association to recognise the Faroe Islands as full members. This was the only international association that the Faroe Islands took part in independent from Denmark until 2021, when the National Union of Faroese Students, *Meginfelag Føroyskra Studenta*, entered the European Students' Union as a full member.

- In 1993, Marita Petersen, a candidate from the Social Democrats, became the first, and to this day, only female prime minister of the Faroe Islands.

- In 2013, the European Union boycotted all trade with the Faroe Islands due to overfishing. This was because the Faroe Islands, in a dispute with the United Kingdom, decided to increase fishing in their waters, as the marcel population had moved from British to Faroese waters. As Denmark was part of the EU, it took part in the boycott. This is the only time that one part of the Danish

Kingdom of Realm has boycotted another part within the Realm. The boycott from the European Union resulted in the Faroe Islands increasing their trade with Russia.

- In 2015, the first openly homosexual MP, Sonja Jógvansdóttir, was elected.

- Since 2017, same-sex marriage has been legal.

- Since 2021, the adoption of children by same-sex female couples has been legalised, while same-sex male couples still haven't gotten this right.

Society

- The Gross Domestic Product growth of the Faroe Islands is among the world's highest.

- About 80% of the population is part of the Faroese Lutheran Church, while another 10% are affiliated with the Christian Brethren movement. The other 10% are either atheists or subscribe to other religions.

- There are approximately 245 yearly marriages and 70 divorces yearly. Two-thirds of the marriages are within the Faroese church.

- The Faroese society is highly digitalised, and many public services are available on an app called Talgildu Føroyar, translated: Digitalised Faroes. This app is connected to people's citizen numbers and allows people to apply for student grants, pensions, funds, etc. They can also register themselves when they move from one municipality to another and when they need to sign their children up for kindergartens. Also, through this app, everyone even has their ancestry tree available.

- Healthcare is free. Dental care is not.

- The average life expectancy is 83,9 years (numbers from 2021); for women, it's 85,6, and for men, it's 82,1 years.

- Education is free, and students receive a monthly student grant for studying.

- On a yearly average, Faroese people consume 6,7 litres of pure alcohol and 59,3 litres of beer (numbers from 2021).

- Criminal rates are among the world's lowest, and the Faroe Islands have no prisons.

- Many Faroe Islanders do not use door keys and do not lock doors, as there is close to no theft.

- Alcohol is legal on all islands except for Lítla Dímun. This is because of the steep mountainsides that make intoxication dangerous.

- Funningur is among the oldest settlements in the Faroe Islands and was settled around 825, which makes it more than three times older than the United States of America.

- During the official Church holidays, drinking or dancing from 9 am to 4 pm is illegal.

- During the church holidays, Maundy Thursday (also known as Holy Thursday) and Good Friday, drinking or dancing is illegal. The dates for these church holidays vary but are always between March 19th and April 22nd.

- Faroese citizens can be issued a red Danish EU passport or a green Faroese non-EU passport.

Industry

- Bakkafrost is a salmon factory. It is the largest fish farming factory and the largest private employer in the Faroe Islands. It is also the third-largest fish farming company in the world.

- The fishing industry contributes to nearly all sales and half of the country's GDP. Tourism is the country's second-largest industry.

- The Áir Whaling Station is one of the world's three remaining historical whaling stations.

- In 2017, the restaurant KOKS received its first Michelin star; in 2019, it was awarded yet another Michelin star.

- In 2022, the two sister restaurants to KOKS, RÆST and ROKS, entered the Michelin Guide.

- In 2017, the tourist bureau Visit Faroe Islands was awarded the Cannes Award for their campaign, Sheep View. Sheep View was an attempt to get Google's attention and to have Google Street View to the Faroe Islands. In Sheep View, panoramic cameras were fitted on sheep's backs and set loose to roam the mountainsides. The sheep could then be trailed like with Street View. One addition to the campaign was a camera placed onto a wheelbarrow in the village of Bø. Those who tried Sheep View could "walk" where the wheelbarrow had been. The campaign resulted in Google Street View being available in the Faroe Islands.

- In 2018, Visit Faroe Islands received another award for the campaign Faroe Islands Translate. Again, this campaign was to get Google's attention and have Faroese as part of Google Translate. In this campaign, Faroese volunteers translated sentences on video recordings, with sentences open for anyone to suggest.

Infrastructure

- The Faroe Islands have four subsea tunnels connecting the islands, which are the only toll roads in the Faroes. These are:

  - *Vágatunnilin* (2002), which connects Vágar and Streymoy.

  - *Norðoyartunnilin* (2005), which connects Borðoy and Eysturoy

  - *Eysturoyartunnilin* (2020), which connects Eysturoy and Streymoy. This tunnel is the world's first subsea tunnel to have its own roundabout and three openings. The *við Streymin Bridge* also connects the two islands since 1973.

- *Sandoyartunnilin* (2023), which connects Streymoy and Sandoy.

- The government plans to build yet another tunnel connecting Sandoy and Suðuroy, the southernmost island. It is expected to be completed by 2030.

- The subsea tunnel, Eysturoyartunnilin, is the first tunnel in the world to have an underwater roundabout.

- As of 2024, there are 26 tunnels, including the subsea tunnels.

- There are approximately 487 kilometres of road, 41 of which are tunnels and subsea tunnels.

- The Streymin Bridge connects the islands of Streymoy and Eysturoy and is said to be "the world's only bridge crossing the Atlantic Ocean."

- It is often said that only three signal lights are on the Faroes. This is not true. There are ten signal lights in total.

- There is a scenic route marked with a buttercup flower. This route leads to the most scenic roads on the islands.

- For every 1.000 people, there are 520 cars, meaning there are over 25.000 cars on the Faroe Islands.

- Buses are free in Tórshavn and Klaksvík.

- About 50% of all energy comes from renewable energy sources.

The goal is to reach 100% by the year 3030.

- Electricity was first introduced in 1921 in Botnur, part of Vágur municipality in Suðuroy.

- A national phone book has been published annually with nearly all the country's phone numbers since the telephone first arrived. With the internet, the use of the phone book saw a decline. When the last edition of the phone book was printed in 2017, it contained the phone numbers of many politicians, including the personal phone number of the Prime Minister.

- Helicopter rides are part of the routes between some of the smaller islands. They can be booked for a relatively small fee when on the route.

- 98% of households have wireless internet.

- High-speed internet has been available on all 18 islands since 3G. Since 2022, the 5G network has had 100% geographic coverage and coverage at sea, spanning 120 kilometres in all directions, meaning there is coverage until you reach international waters.

- A speed test conducted in March 2023, using 5G, was the fastest measured connection ever recorded in Europe.

- Because of the fast internet connection, the Faroese telecom, Føroya Tele, will provide internet to SaxaVord, the UK Space Port, in the Shetland Islands.

Geography

- The Faroe Islands archipelago is made of 18 islands. Because of their elongated shape, you can never be farther than 5km from the ocean.

- The islands are made from volcanic eruptions.

- Only a handful of warm springs have been found in the Faroes. The first discovered, Varmakelda, is believed to have been known since Viking times and was first mentioned in writing in 1673. It was believed that this spring had healing powers. It is approximately 18 degrees Celsius.

- 17 of 18 islands are inhabited, while the 18th island, Lítla Dímun, has not been inhabited since Viking times. Simultaneously, Lítla Dímun is the only island that is privately owned.

- Although the Faroe Islands are in the GMT 0 time zone, the westernmost island, Mykines, is partly in GMT -1. This means that Mykines is technically in two time zones. The border between these two time zones exactly hits the stream that runs through the island's only village.

- You can see the Northern Lights in the winter.

- There are three places where the magnetic field is weaker than in other places in the Faroes; in the fjord between Fugloy and Sandoy, in the fjord between Skúvoy and Sandoy, and in the waters south of Sumba, in a place called Sumbiarsteinur. The magnetic field is believed to be weakened because of the strong current; so weak that weak compasses do not work.

- Cape Enniberg is the highest sea cliff in Europe and one of the highest sea cliffs in the world.

- Klæmintsgjógv, Hestur, is the largest sea cave in the world.

- The Faroe Islands have often had all four distinct seasons in a single day.

- The average temperature is 7 degrees Celsius.

- The warmer months of May to August are the best time to visit the Faroe Islands.

Nature

- It is widely believed that no trees are native to the Faroe Islands. This is not true. Here are some of the original tree species of the Faroe Islands:

  - Juniper (Juniperus Communis) was widespread across the islands but rapidly declined when the Norwegian hares were introduced in 1855. Today, Juniper is only common on Svínoy, while it is rare on all other islands.

  - Dwarf willow (Salix herbacea)

  - Woolly willow (Salix lanata)

- Tea-leaved willow (*Salix phylicifolia*)

- Arctic willow (*Salix arctica*)

- Common hazel (*Corylus avellana*) *Disappeared around the year 1200. The Vikings might have introduced it.

- Dwarf birch (*Betula nana*) was native to the Faroes until around 8.000 BC.

- Downy Birch (Betula *pubescens*) disappeared when people settled in the Faroes.

- Driftwood that washes up on the Faroese shores is primarily from Siberia, secondly Canada, and thirdly Norway.

Animals

- The Faroe Islands used to have white-tailed eagles on some high mountain peaks. Some placenames are named after eagles, indicating their residence, and legends tell of tragic incidents where the eagles have taken small children. The last white-tailed eagle was shot in the early 1900s.

- The White Pead Raven, or the White Raven, as the islanders know it, was the same species as the regular black raven that still lives in the Faroes. It only lived in the Faroe Islands; the last raven was seen in 1948 in Nólsoy. However, scientists speculate that the DNA could still be carried with the current breed and hope that the Faroe Islands one day will have the White Raven as one of its local species.

- Frogs were first introduced in Nólsoy in 2002; in 2004, they had their first offspring. Nólsoy is the only island that has frogs.

- There are plenty of seals which, during the summer mornings, can be seen resting on the rocky beaches around the islands. According to the Faroese myth, the seals are people who have committed suicide by throwing themselves into the sea from the high mountainous cliffs or fishermen who have drowned while at sea. From this belief, it is said that on January 6th, the seals come to land at midnight, taking off their hides and then taking the shape of people. On this night, they dance until sunrise.

- Drunnhvíti, The European storm petrel, reciedes in Nólsoy, Mykines and on some other islands. Nólsoy is the largest breeding area for this bird species in the world.

- Skúgvur, the Great Skua, recedes in high numbers on the island of Skúvoy, which is the world's largest breeding area for this species. When people first settled on the Faroe Islands, there were so many birds on the island that the island itself was named after them.

- In 1855, Norwegian hares were set loose into the Faroese mountains. They were introduced as a new food resource. When it was introduced, it was brown, but after some 50 years, the hare had adapted to its new surroundings. Now the hare is brown in the summer and grey in the winter.

- Even though the Faroe Islands have legal whale hunts, there is no such thing as a whaling season, and whales are not being hunted commercially.

- Official records of all whale hunts date back to 1584 and are considered particularly reliable from 1709 onward. These statistics are considered the oldest hunting statistics in the world.

- The Faroe Islands means "Sheep Islands" (plural), while the Scottish island Soay means "Sheep Island" (singular). The sheep on Soay is the closest related breed to the original Faroese sheep.

- The Faroese horse is the world's most endangered horse species.

- Faroese for Albatross is Súlukongur, which means *the King of the Gannets*. This comes from the 1950s when an albatross nested among the gannets in Mykines for some years.

- In 2023, birdwatchers noticed that the gannet's eye colour had switched from bright blue to black. It's unclear why this has happened, but since 2021, the gannet has been infected with bird flu, which is believed to be the cause of the changed colour, though this has yet to be confirmed.

Chapter Sixteen
The Unique Travel Guide

The Faroe Islands, brimming with vibrant creativity and innovation, offer diverse cultural experiences in music, art, literature, crafts, design, and gastronomy. Traditions from the Faroe Islands have been preserved while allowing new creative forces to flourish.

Despite centuries of isolation, the Faroe Islands have developed a distinct and rich culture. Because of the relative isolation, access to instruments, tools, and materials was previously very limited. As a result, storytelling, ballads, and the distinctive chain dance play an essential role in Faroese cultural heritage, and singing is deeply rooted in Faroese culture.

Over the last centuries, as the Faroes have become increasingly more connected to the rest of the world, the cultural scene has evolved and grown and is still flourishing. However, artists in all fields continue to draw inspiration from the riches of Faroese nature and tradition.

In this chapter, I will provide you with the best recommendations on what to see and do during your stay, many of which are amongst the cheapest attractions within the country.

Chapter Seventeen
Art, Music and Culture

The Faroe Islands have a very diverse and vivid cultural scene. Music and the arts are flourishing, and you can see artists in music and the fine arts represented worldwide. Music especially has been very well represented; in television series, videogames and so forth, some musicians have even been signed by labels such as Universal Records.

Why that is, well, that hasn't been investigated, but if you look at habits and tastes among Faroese youth, it is common to see original paintings in homes, even in the homes of people in their late teenage years.

Music is an essential part of Faroese culture and part of the morning ritual in every public school, where students and teachers sing songs each morning before class. Also, in the olden days, the tradition of chain dancing and singing within the Faroese homes was a natural part of everyday life. Today, this tradition has vanished, but the chain dancing and singing of old hymns and ballads have remained a part of the public-school curriculum.

Music and art are also part of the curriculum, ensuring that anyone, regardless of their interest, will be introduced to music and art. Also, the music training system is available nationwide, where public school students can be taught an instrument after the demanded classes. Following this, students who wish to pursue a career in music can take an upper-secondary diploma in music, which is inspired by the music conservatory traditions and gives access to most of the world's conservatories. After finishing this diploma, they can continue their studies at the University of the Faroe Islands, offering a Bachelor of Arts program in music production and theory as a Bachelor of Arts program in creative writing.

Through the years, many music contests have been held annually, where participants can win a tour abroad or are given the opportunity to perform at the annual music festivals.

In this section, you will be provided with the most recommended places to visit or experience if you are interested in music, arts, or culture.

Summertónar

The Composers' and Songwriters' Festival, Summartónar, offers various concerts throughout the summer. The concerts are held around the country and in different settings, from the heart of Tórshavn to the outer islands such as Svínoy, onboard the old schooner Norðlýsið, and within the sea caves of Hestur.

If you're looking for a unique experience, it is worth looking at the Summartónar programme.

See more: www.summartonar.fo

G! Festival. Photo by Rúni í Múla.

The G! festival

The Faroe Islands' most exciting and culturally challenging music festival, always guaranteeing a broad and diverse range of enjoyable musical and cultural elements. The festival is in Syðrugøta, a small village surrounded by high mountain tops and a sandy beach. The festival is typically held in mid-June.

If you're looking for a vibrant musical experience with a surprisingly good atmosphere and the best of what a music experience can offer the G! Festival is the number one recommendation.

See more at: www.gfestival.fo

Hoyma: Home Concerts

Hoyma is a concept where concerts are held in people's homes. It is very similar to concepts such as Sofar Sounds and Sofa Concerts, but unlike Sofar Sounds, anyone can buy tickets to the venues. Hoyma is held locally in Syðrugøta, home to the G! festival, and the founders of Hoyma are the same as the founders of the festival.

Concerts are held sporadic throughout the year and are predominately held off-season.

In 2021, Lonely Planet included the Faroe Islands as one of the best destinations on the annual Best in Travel list. The reason for being included on this list was partly because of the Hoyma concerts and Heimablídni (see page 147).

Tickets and information on the venues can be found on the website www.hoyma.fo.

Museums of Fine Art

The National Museum of Art is in the heart of Tórshavn, on the outskirts of the central park, which has many planted trees. This museum offers the best of art ever made in the Faroes. With household names such as Sámal J. Mikines and Tróndur Patursson, you can see some of the original paintings that have made these artists famous worldwide.

Address: Gundadalsvegur 9, Tórshavn
Phone: (+298) 22 35 79
e-mail: info@art.fo
Website: www.art.fo

An alternative visit worth doing is going to the Art Gallery on Sandur, Sandoy, a private collection donated to the village by art collector Sofus Olsen, who also paid for the impressive gallery building. This museum is on the same level as the national museum, showcasing many impressive works by some of the most prominent Faroese artists.

Address: Áarbøur 11, Sandur
Phone: (+298) 21 19 24
e-mail: info@listasavnid.fo
Website: www.listasavnid.fo

Heystfagnaður and Sjómannadagar

Each fall in Eiði, the village hosts a local festival focusing on agriculture and farming. Here, people compete with performing tasks from the traditional Faroese way of life, such as slaughtering sheep or seeing who can lift a sack of potatoes the longest. Many old traditions are on display for anyone to enjoy.

For many, the Heystfagnaður festival is perceived as a counterculture to modern life in Tórshavn, though it is trendy for people from Tórshavn to attend at this venue.

During the festival, there is an animal zoo with domestic animals, you can buy roots and vegetables grown locally, the local museums and the church are open, and the boat houses are all filled with different activities; beer is served for the grownups, and there are many activities for children.

Heystfagnaður is typically held in mid-October, and you can stay oriented by following their Facebook page, "Heystfagnaður á Eiði."

Another similar village festival is Sjómannadagar, held annually in Klaksvík in August. Much like the Heystfagnaður, Sjómannadagar is a local village festival focusing on fisheries and everything related to fisheries.

Ólavsøka

Ólavsøka is the largest festival in the Faroe Islands and is held annually in Tórshavn on the 28th and 29th of July. It is one of the oldest festivals, celebrated annually since around 1300 when the Norwegian church made it a church holiday in remembrance of King Olaf II Haraldsson of Norway (Olaf the Holy).

It is often claimed that Ólavsøka is the Faroese national holiday, although Faroe Island does not technically have one. Still, many perceive it as such, and it is often called such in books and articles about the Faroe Islands. If you ask someone on the street what the national holiday is, they will most likely say Ólavsøka, as it is a commonly held belief. This is perhaps understandable because it is a season of great significance, as the Faroese parliament, Løgtingið, has its yearly formal assembly on Ólavsøka.

On Ólavsøka, the streets of Tórshavn are brimming with people from all over the country, wearing traditional Faroese costumes. People living abroad are often returning home at this time, and because of its popularity, many tourists can also be seen during this time.

If you visit Tórshavn during Ólavsøka, you can enjoy various art exhibitions, open bars, street food, lotteries, rowing boat races, parades, choir singing, community singing, traditional Faroese chanting and dancing, and much more.

It is essential to know that you must secure your accommodation beforehand since it can be hard to get accommodation during these days.

The Knitting Festival

Each year around April, the knitting festival, Bindifestivalurin, is held in Fuglafjørður. This is a significant event, mainly focusing on knitting, spinning, and anything made from wool. The festival contains lecturers, hiking trips, and a wide range of workshops. The festival itself is arranged by locals and is tied to the local home industry, which has a shop in one of the village's old buildings and is run by volunteer workers.

The festival attracts people from the Faroes and has visitors from all over the world, many of whom either participate or hold the workshops and lectures.

The festival is usually held over three days, and visitors can buy single-day tickets or tickets for the whole festival.

See dates, prices and more: www.bindifestival.com

Heimavirki: Home-Made Goods

Heimavirki translates into Home Industry and is a well-known way of buying and selling Faroese-made products such as sweaters and other home-produced goods. These craft shops are run by volunteer workers, local to the different areas, and usually, these workers are also some of the producers of the products sold in these shops.

Føroya Heimavirkisfelag
Address: Niels Finsens Gøta 7, Tórshavn

Lávusarhús
Address: Á bakka 2, Leirvík

Norðoya Heimavirki
Address: Biskupsgøta 11, Klaksvík

Ribarhús & Piddasahandil
Address: Í støð 14, Fuglafjørður

Suðuroyar Heimavirki
Address: Vágsvegur 47, Vágur

Chapter Eighteen

History and Historic Sites

Despite having existed for only a little more than a thousand years and lacking written historical documents, the Faroe Islands are not poor in history.

Historic houses have been preserved throughout the country, and archaeological excavations have shown old settlements throughout many villages.

In many villages, statues have been put up that tell of the many myths told locally. You can find the Selkie in Mikladalur, the Nix in Lake Leitisvatn, the Merman in Elduvík and Fuglafjørður, and the Shepherd of Sondum in Miðvágur.

The most historical places are Kirkjubø, Tinganes in Tórshavn, the old farm of Hoyvík, the old Fort in Tórshavn, and the World War II ruins that are scattered around, especially on the island of Vágar.

There are also a handful of abandoned villages you can visit by hiking. A list of the villages is also included in this chapter.

Historical Museums

A great way of experiencing the Faroe Islands is by visiting the museums. Although the main state-funded museums have merged in recent years, there are a few other mueseums that are either privately funded or funded by the municipalities. Here are a few recommendations that are worth a visit and, perhaps, more interesting than other museums you can also find across the country.

The National Museum

Tjóðsavnið, or the National Museum, has a permanent and open-air exhibition with interchangeable instalments. Here, you can get a glimpse of the history, culture, and nature of the Faroe Islands.

You can expect to see old Faroese clothing, the traditional Faroese clinker boat, silver coins and other archaeological excavation findings, stuffed examples of extinct animal species, old photos, stones and gems from nature, and much more.

Address: Brekkutún 6, Hoyvík
Phone: (+298) 31 80 76
e-mail: savn@savn.fo
Website: www.tjodsavnid.fo

SagaMuseum

SagaMuseum in Vestmanna is a wax museum that evolves around the history and sagas of the Faroe Islands. In the museum, several realistic-looking wax figures are placed in surroundings that either reference places and surroundings from history or exact copies of historical places around the islands. The museum visit is a virtual tour through time, from the Viking Age until today, and it is a great introduction to the history of the Faroe Islands as told through the Færeyinga Saga, myth and documented history. Museum visitors can purchase tickets for a reduced price for the boat tour to the Vestmanna Bird Cliffs and vice versa.

Address: Fjarðavegur 2, Vestmanna
Phone: (+298) 47 15 00
e-mail: touristinfo@olivant.fo
website: www.visit-vestmanna.com

The War Museum

The World War II Museum is located by the airport in Vágar. It is an old Military building used by the British soldiers in the area with the most military activity. The museum collects artefacts from the war, and presentations and stories are often told from the war times.

Address: Varðagøta 61, Sørvágur
Phone: (+298) 22 19 40
e-mail: krigssavnid@ww2.fo
Website: www.ww2.fo

Viking settlements

In Leirvík and Kvívík, you can visit some well-preserved ruins that have been dug out in the two villages. Both places are free and open to visitors.

Both settlements are tiny and have described signs about the respective areas and what was found during the excavations. If you go to Kvívík, you can also enjoy the small, cosy village, famous for its tiny houses with grass-covered roofs and the stream that runs through it.

How to get there

When you look out towards the sea, the Kvívík settlement is down by the shore, on the right-hand side. The Leirvík settlement is in a field above the main road right after you pass the petrol station after arriving through the tunnel.

The library room in the King's farm. Photo by Mélanie Arouk on Unsplash.

Kirkjubø

Arguably one of the most important sites of the Middle Ages, Kirkjubøur is one of the most historic sites of the Faroe Islands. Here, you can see one of the world's oldest wooden houses, the ruined Magnus Cathedral, the oldest church of the Faroes and the cave where the Norwegian king, Sverrir Sigurðsson, is said to have lived.

Visiting Kirkjubø is always a recommendation and can be done with or without a local guide. For the ultimate experience, booking a guide, preferably someone local, is recommended. If you decide to use the local farmer as a guide, it is one of the **cheapest tourist attractions** in the Faroe Islands and **contributes to the farm's economy**.

See more: www.patursson.fo

Tinganes and Reyn: The Old District of Tórshavn

Tinganes and Reyn are the oldest and most historic places in Tórshavn. The iconic old wooden buildings, many of which have grass roofs, are painted in a traditional Faroese style, and they are the cosiest district in town.

Tinganes is where the old Viking assembly was. Back then, it shared the same name as the Icelandic Altingið but was later renamed Løgtingið. On this site, many sentences were made, people were executed and drowned (see pages 18 - 21), and new laws were made.

Tinganes was also the trading centre during the time of the King's Monopoly Store, and the Danish officials had their main offices there.

In 1673, Tinganes was set on fire, and many of the old houses that used to stand there burned to the ground. Therefore, many of the buildings that are still standing have been built in the years after.

Today, Tinganes serves as parliamentary buildings where politicians and public offices are hosted.

Questo's Ghosts of Tórshavn: The Lost Commandant. Photo by Terji Beder.

Ghosts of Tórshavn: The Lost Commandant

This self-guided tour takes you through the most haunted, historic, and scenic places in Tórshavn and is amongst the cheapest tourist attractions in the Faroe Islands.

The game is a mix between an escape room and geo catching, where you wander through the streets of Tórshavn, solving riddles and cracking codes to progress in the game.

See more: www.questoapp.com or by downloading the Questo app on App Store or Google Play. Prices are available on the app.

Skansin Fort. Photo by Papa_rapa on Pixabay

Skansin: The Old Fort

First built in 1580, the old fort, Skansin, is the oldest preserved military installation on the Faroe Islands. Over time, it has served several different purposes: as a prison, for protection from private ships and invaders, and during World War II, as the main quarters for the British military.

Through time, the fort has been rebuilt and expanded, and initially, it was one of three forts of its kind in Tórshavn. Today, the Skansin Fort is the only fort still standing and serves as a free park area that anyone can visit freely.

Koltur Island

Second to Lítla Dímun, Koltur is the most isolated island in the Faroes. The old village with stone houses with grass roofs is still standing and can be visited. Koltur also has a small sandy beach and a modern farmhouse where the island's only two residents live.

Koltur is the only national park in the Faroes, and in the near future, all sheep will be removed from the island, letting nature flourish without any animal interference. Additionally, the Faroese government plans to establish a research station on the island, which will be built in a traditional Faroese way. When the research station is established, Koltur becomes more accessible as a tourist attraction.

How to get there

There is no ferry connection to Koltur, which makes it hard to reach. However, there are private options, such as booking a day trip to the island, although it can be rather expensive.

Áir Whaling Station

In Áir, between Hósvík and Hvalvík, there are many tiny red houses. This used to be a whaling station where industrialised whaling used to take place in the olden days. Now, the station is marked as an industrial heritage site and is part of the National Museum, and you can visit on-site and get a guided tour.

The whaling station is one of three in the world and is the only station still standing in the northern hemisphere.

You can visit the whaling station without payment, but if you wish to tour the site to access the many industrial buildings, you must take the tour.

The whaling station is open from 10 am to 5 pm on Saturdays and Sundays from mid-June to mid-August, and prices for a guided tour.

Prices for adults: 80 DKK
Prices for students and seniors: 50 DKK
Prices per person in a group of 10 or more: 50 DKK

Children have free entry.

Abandoned Villages

Throughout the Faroe Islands, many villages have been abandoned through time. Most of these villages have been demolished because of tragic deaths, where, in many cases, all the men from the village have been lost at sea. Since this was before roads were built, they are only accessible by foot.

- Skarð, Kunoy

  It is only accessible with a paid guide. Contact Visit Norðoy to purchase a guided hike.

- Blankskáli, Kalsoy

  It is not accessible by foot but can be reached by boat.

- Múli, Borðoy

  It is accessible by car.

- Víkar, Vágar,

  It is accessible by foot, starting from Gásadalur, although it is considered a strenuous hike. An information sign in Gásadalur will direct you to your route.

- Slættanes, Vágar

  It is accessible by foot by heading north from Oyragjógv.

- Korndalur, Nólsoy

  It is easily accessible by foot, near Nólsoy village.

- Fámará, Suðuroy

It is accessible by car, though the road is very rough. It is not advised to drive there without having four-wheel drive, preferably a car intended for off-roading.

- Víkarbyrgi, Suðuroy
  It is accessible by car, although the road is narrow.

- Akraberg, Suðuroy
  It is accessible by car, although the road is narrow.

There are many other abandoned villages, but most were abandoned so many years ago that all traces of human activity, except for the imprints left by the cultivation of the fields, have been lost. In some places, however, all human traces have been completely lost and are no longer visible without specialised technology.

Chapter Nineteen

Restaurants and Dining

Although groceries and other food might seem expensive, fine dining is relatively cheap in the Faroe Islands. In Tórshavn, there is a wide range of high-end restaurants. Compared with the prices of regular take-away, fine dining can be considered relatively cheap, and if you compare the prices, it might be worth considering a finer meal than going to Burger King, etc.

If you prefer a dining experience with fish, steak, high-quality pizza, street food or traditional Faroese food, Tórshavn has you covered. Most restaurants can be found in the town's centre, and many of the more exclusive restaurants are in small cottages near Tinganes, which only adds to the authentic experience.

Though it can be harder to find a good-quality meal in rural areas, there are a few places worth a visit, some of which are at least of the same quality as the high-end restaurants in the capital.

This section includes a list of recommended dining places and a description of each place's offerings.

Heimablídni: Dining in Faroese Homes

The most authentic food experience you can have while visiting the Faroe Islands is to dine with the concept of Heimablídni, home hospitality.

A concept that has proven increasingly popular is the home dining concept Heimablídni. With this concept, locals invite people to dine in their homes with food the hosts have prepared. There are many such places where you can eat, and the food served is as varied and authentic as the hosts themselves and the homes they live in. Because this concept is held in people's homes and by the homeowners, different offers aren't always available, but

A list of places to dine can be found on www.eatlocal.fo, and you can book your reservation there.

Additionally, there is another place where you can eat in the same manner, though it isn't listed on the website mentioned above.

Karlsá Heimablídni, in Klaksvík, makes pizza like no other. They have a separate little shed where guests can eat and have private time, and pizza is served ad libitum.

Address: Karlsvegur 6, Klaksvík
Phone: (+298) 22 44 34
e-mail: karlsa@karlsa.fo

ROKS and RÆST

The two restaurants, ROKS and RÆST, are sister restaurants to the famous Faroese restaurant KOKS which has been awarded two Michelin stars. Since KOKS moved to Greenland a few years ago, ROKS and RÆST have been included in the Micheline Guide.

Situated in small cottage-like houses in the old part of Tórshavn, these two restaurants serve very high-quality meals in a cosy environment.

Suppose you'd like to try a modern take on traditional Faroese fermented food. In that case, RÆST is the place for you, and if you'd like to try food that has been caught and harvested locally but that hasn't been part of the traditional Faroese cuisine, such as Faroese lobsters and sea urchins, then ROKS is the place for you.

Either way, both restaurants are well worth a visit, which the Michelin Guide also suggests, and both restaurants serve the best wine you can find on the Faroe Islands.

RÆST's address: Gongin 8, Tórshavn
ROKS's address: Gongin 5, Tórshavn

See more at: □www.raest.fo and www.roks.fo

Photo by Elina Sazonova on Pexels.

Fiskastykkið

In Miðvágur, the restaurant Fiskastykki resides in some old factory buildings used to dry fish. Fiskastykki is the Faroese word for the outdoor area where people used to sun dry fish before piling them up in the warehouses.

Today, these surroundings host a luxurious and cosy café, serving seafood from arguably the best and freshest ingredients.

Address: Úti á Bakka 12, Sandavágur
Phone: (+298) 25 06 00
Website: www.fiskastykkid.fo

Restaurant Muntra

In Fuglafjørður, there is a restaurant that serves a wide range of meals. The restaurant is open every day year-round between 12 a.m. and 10 p.m. but is typically closed in January and February.

The food from this restaurant isn't trying to impress. Still, it relies on a solid traditional way of cooking, with over 40 years of experience and with regular customers since the restaurant first opened.

Restaurant Muntra is most famous for its fish soup, made from dried fish heads delivered from a drying factory in the neighbouring village of Leirvík. These fishheads give an intense aroma and a tasty fish flavour, which you cannot find anywhere else on the Faroe Islands.

Address: Toftagøta 1 A, Fuglafjørður
Phone: (+298) 44 40 81

Vegetarian and Vegan options

Finding vegetarian or vegan restaurants in the Faroe Islands can be challenging, but you can always ask if they serve anything vegan at any restaurant. But, there are some places where they do serve vegan or vegetarian dishes. Here is a list:

- Sirkus, Tórshavn

- Fiskastykkið, Sandavágur

- Café Fríða, Klaksvík

- Kafe Umami, Tórshavn

- Suppugarðurin, Tórshavn

- Etika Sushi, Tórshavn

- Systrar, Tórshavn

- Bitin, Tórshavn

Additionally, Burger King and Sunset Boulevard have vegetarian options.

Also, most supermarkets have vegan and vegetarian options if you prefer preparing your own food.

Other recommended dining experiences

In Tórshavn:

- The Tarv, *steakhouse*

- Áarstova, *steakhouse*

- Barbara Fishhouse, *fish restaurant*

- Skeiva Pakkhús, *Italian food*

- Etika, *sushi*

- Suppugarðurin, *traditional Japanese ramen*

- Reyðleyk, *pizza*

- Haps, *burger joint*

- Ástaklokkan, *micro restaurant*

Outside Tórshavn:

- Amarant, *bakery and pizza*, Klaksvík

- Rose's Café, *restaurant*, Ljósá

Both in and outside Tórshavn, it's worth to keep an eye out for food trucks, as this is the only way street-food is being served. This is, however, only during the summertime, though some food trucks can be seen in the early spring to late fall.

Chapter Twenty

Distilleries and Breweries

Over the past 20 years, there has been a shift in mentality when it comes to alcohol in the Faroe Islands. Here, you can see a significant development in the production and enjoyment of local goods. Interest associations, especially whiskey associations, have taken over the islands, and in recent years, we have seen a relatively large number of new breweries and distilleries. Everything is connected, and these ripple effects are visible in a society with such a limited customer base as the Faroese. The new breweries have challenged the more established ones, which has resulted in the old mammoth in the capital, Restorff Brewery, going bankrupt.

The connection between beer enthusiasts and breweries is evident in the same way as with spirits production. Here, for example, you can see that many of the leading whiskey enthusiasts who have helped build the enthusiast association Einmalt go to both Einars Distillery and Fair Isles Distillery again. In the same way, it is with Brett, the beer enthusiast association, where many of the same people return to the OY brewery.

Whisky Storage. Photo by Rúni í Múla.

If you want to find out about events for beer, wine or spirits enthusiasts, you should find out about the associations. Often, these are not so organized but are run by enthusiasts on a hobby level, typically on Facebook pages and groups and, to a limited extent, also on Instagram. Therefore, all those interested should apply to the associations on social media.

- **Brett**

  The Faroese Craftbeer Union

- **EinMalt**

  The Primary Whisky Enthusiast Association

- **NorðMalt**

  Whisky Enthusiast Association in the Northern Islands

- **Vínkúllarnir**

  Pop-up winebar

Rúsan, the Monopoly Store

Apart from bars and restaurants and the breweries, the Rúsan monopoly is the only place you can buy alcohol in the Faroe Islands. Rúsan has all the shops around the country where alcohol can be purchased.

Here is an overview of the shops, their addresses, and their opening hours. Please note, however, that the opening hours can change and that you should always orient yourself on the website www.rusan.fo.

- **Rúsan in Runavík**
  Heiðavegur 25, Saltangará
  Monday to Thursday: 1 pm to 5:30 pm
  Friday: 10 am to 5:30 pm
  Saturday: 10 am to 2 pm

- **Rúsan in Klaksvík**
  Sævargøta 6, Klaskvík
  Monday to Thursday: 1 pm to 5:30 pm
  Friday: 10 am to 5:30 pm
  Saturday: 10 am to 2 pm

- **Rúsan in Tvøroyri**
  Trongisvágsvegur 20, Trongisvágur
  Monday to Thursday: 1 pm to 5:30 pm
  Friday: 12 am to 5:30 pm
  Saturday: 10 am to 14 pm

- **Rúsan in Miðvágur**
  Skaldavegur 5, Miðvágur
  Monday to Thursday: 2 pm to 5:30 pm
  Friday: 12 am to 5:30 pm
  Saturday: 10 am to 2 pm

- **Rúsan in Sandur**
  Heimasandsvegur 58, Sandur
  Monday to Friday: 2 pm to 5:30 pm
  Saturdau: 10 am to 2 pm

- **Rúsan in Norðskáli**
  Svartheyggj 2, Norðskáli
  Monday to Friday: 1 pm to 5:30 pm
  Saturday: 10 am to 2 pm

- **Rúsan in Vestmanna**
  Niðari Vegur 81, Vestmanna
  Thursday to Friday: 4 pm to 6 pm
  Satyrday: 12 am to 2 pm

Faer Isle Distillery

With its distillery and visitor centre located in Vestmanna and its warehouse (still under construction) in the mountains between Vestmanna and Kvívík, the Faer Isle Distillery is amongst the world's youngest Whisky distilleries. Though the distillery was only founded in 2019, it produces several handcrafted, high-quality spirits using local ingredients, such as herbs, seaweed, clear mountain water and water from a subsea tunnel. The Faroese climate makes for ideal whisky maturation in the wet and salty wind.

The Distillery Tour is amongst the **cheapest tourist attractions in the Faroe Islands** and can be booked by phone or e-mail:

Phone: (+298) 77 90 00
e-mail: info@faer.fo
Website: www.faer.io
Address: Fjarðavegur 3, Vestmanna

Spirits can be bought at the distillery's visitors' centre.

Føroya Bjór Brewery and Einar's Distillery

Founded in 1888, Føroya Bjór is the oldest still-running Faroese brewery. It makes a wide selection of products but is most famous for its traditional lagers, many of which have won prestigious prizes for their high quality. The brewery is family-owned and is run by the family's third generation. In recent years, the brewery has introduced soft drinks and alcohol-free beer. It has also expanded with a distillery named Einar's Distillery after the current owner of Føroya Bjórr, Einar Waag.

Guided tours to the brewery and distillery can be booked by phone or e-mail:

Phone: (+298) 47 54 54
E-mail: fb@foroyabjor.fo
Website: www.bjor.fo and www.einarsdistillery.fo
Address: Klakksvíksvegur 19, Klaksvík

Spirits and beer can be bought at the visitors' centre.

Biskupskelda Brewery

The microbrewery Biskupskelda aims to bring life to old tales from the Faroese myth. Its beer is inspired by old and local folk tales.

It was founded in 2021 in Vágur, Suðuroy, and as of 2022, it has ten different types of beer. Five can be bought at the Monopoly store, while the other five can only be bought at the brewery.

Brewing started in rented facilities, but in 2022, the brewery bought a historic building that will serve as its primary production building and visitor centre. Until the building is finished, Biskupskelda offers guided beer walks in the village of Vágur and hikes in nature. If you wish to visit the brewery, you must do so by e-mail.

e-mail: biskupskelda@gmail.com
website: www.biskupskelda.fo
Address: Vágsvegur 107B, Vágur

Beer can be bought in the visitors' centre. Special brews are only available at the brewery, and can not be bought in Rúsan.

OY Brewpub and Take-away!

With its combined brewpub and takeaway concept in the same factory building where the beer is brewed, OY is arguably the hippest of all the breweries. You can book a tour through the brewery, have a meal, or just go for a casual pint at their site. On weekends, they often host concerts and other events, such as stand-up comedy.

Oy was founded in 2021 by Faroese beer enthusiasts with experience from Okkara and people from the restaurant and hospitality business.

Beers from OY can be bought at the Monopoly store, but if you visit their site, many more options are kept on tap. And a visit to the brewery is worth a visit.

Phone: (+298) 78 22 00
e-mail: oy@oy.fo
website: www.oy.fo
Address: Falkavegur 4, Tórshavn

Beer can be bought at the OY shop and Bar.

Chapter Twenty-One

Exclusive and Authentic High-end Souvenirs

If you wish to bring home something from your stay in the Faroe Islands, nothing is better than buying a souvenir that you'll be happy to have bought as a souvenir and an item you can use. Here are some recommendations that will make you happier with your bought memories.

Knitwear

If you'd like to purchase a Faroese knitted sweater, traditional or modern, there are a wide number of shops you can go to. In Tórshavn, you'll find *Sirri*, *Shishabrand*, *Einstakt* and *Guðrun & Guðrun*. In Toftir, you can visit *Navia*, which also has a shop in SMS, the shopping centre in Tórshavn. *Snældan* has a shop in Strendur but also in Tórshavn. In Klaksvík, there's also a shop called *Hjá Vimu*.

Alternatively, you can buy home-knitted sweaters from one of the home craft shops (see page 130) or secondhand.

Leirlist Ceramics

At Leirlist Ceramics, you can buy handmade Japanese-inspired pottery made from clay infused with sand, iron and other things found in the Faroese mountains. Leirlist Ceramics has a small workshop and shop in a small basement in the heart of Tórshavn, and there is a small self-managed shop where you can take what is presented on a wooden shelf by leaving your payment in the mailbox. To make this purchase, you must, of course, have cash.

Address: Sjúrðargøta 16, Tórshavn
Phone: (+298) 25 32 51
e-mail: leirlist@olivant.fo

Fine Art

Bring a part of Faroese culture with you by buying an authentic Faroese painting at one of the art shops or purchasing an art poster at one of the galleries.

If this idea sounds appealing, a great tip is to visit *Steinprent Galleries* in Tórshavn, where original lithographs can be bought cheaply. Steinprent is affordable and one of Europe's highest-quality lithographic printing presses presenting contemporary fine art by Faroese and Scandinavian artists.

Another way to buy art is to visit *Myndlist*, *Glarsmiðjan*, or *Gallarí Havnará*. These galleries are more expensive and focus mainly on acrylic and oil paintings.

If you want something special for the lowest cost, visit the *National Museum of Art* or the *Art Museum in Sandur*. Both have art posters and postcards with famous Faroese paintings.

Book shops

A book is always a good memory to have, and here you can buy Faroese books written in English, which might otherwise be difficult to find in the rest of the world. If you wish to buy a book, you can do so at the Airport in Vágar, or you can visit some local bookshops, such as *Rit & Rák* in the shopping centre in Tórshavn, or at *Gamli Bókahandil*, the old bookstore in the centre of Tórshavn.

Beer and Spirits

Though it may not be a lasting memory, you may wish to purchase a sample beer six-pack from one of the local breweries or a bottle of alcohol, such as whisky, gin or vodka, from one of the local distilleries. That way, you can enjoy more of the Faroes and even share your experiences with your friends over a beer or drink.

Østrøm

Østrøm is a shop that focuses on high-end quality crafts from the Faroes. You can get Faroese-made jewellery, pottery, designer clothes, household goods carved from driftwood, etc.

Address: Skálatrøð 18, Tórshavn
Phone: (+298) 26 05 60
e-mail: hj@ostrom.fo

Chapter Twenty-Two

Well-known Gems in Nature

In the last 10 years or so, tourism has been booming in the Faroe Islands, attracting television and advertising companies to make commercials on many of the sites. Travel agencies not only in the Faroes but also in other countries have been advertising using many of these sites. Because of this, these areas have seen an increasing number of tourists visiting all year round.

Some places have become so popular that it has damaged the grass and many of the old walking paths, some of which are hundreds, perhaps thousands of years old. But in reaction to the stressed nature, the Faroese authorities, in collaboration with the national tourist bureau, Visit Faroe Islands, have made walking paths to reduce the said stress.

Therefore, it is of the utmost importance that anyone visiting any of these places stick to the paths marked on the trails and respect all the signs that have been put up. If not, it can harm the natural area, birdlife, and so on.

The Lake Above the Ocean. Photo by Rúni í Múla.

The Lake Above the Ocean

One of the most visited tourist attractions and one of the most iconic sceneries in the Faroe Islands is, without a doubt, the site at Trælanípa. Trælanípa is the name of the cliffs that reside outside Lake Leitisvatn, best known as the lake above the sea.

It is only a five-minute drive from the airport in Vágar and a 45-minute walk from where you park your car. However, visiting this site demands a fee of 200 DKK, and for an additional 250 DKK, you can get a guide to show you around, which is the recommended way to go.

Múlafossur Waterfall. Photo by Tomáš Malík on Pexels.

Múlafossur

In this scenic area, with the waterfall falling directly into the Atlantic Ocean and the small quiet village of Gásadalur resting above, you can take one of the Faroe Islands' best pictures on your travels.

This site is the most visited in the Faroes and has been part of many commercials worldwide.

The waterfall is only a ten-minute drive from the Airport in Vágar and is accessible by a short walk from the main road.

If you go to Gásadalur, signs will lead you to it.

The Giant and the Hag. Photo by Lachlan Gowen on Unsplash.

The Giant and the Hag

The two mythical sea stacks, the Giant and the Hag stand on the sea below the high cliffs, frozen in stone in a failed attempt to pull the Faroe Islands to Iceland. According to legend, they couldn't pull the Faroe Islands all the way to Iceland before the sun rose, turning them into stone.

These sea stacks are probably one of the most famous folktales from the Faroes and can be seen from the village Tjørnuvík or from the narrow road between Eiði and Gjógv (see the Buttercup routes).

If you decide to drive on this Buttercup Route, you should stop by the telescope, where you can investigate them further.

Saksun Beach. Photo by Rúni í Múla.

Saksun and Saksun Beach

Saksun is a small village known for its beautiful natural surroundings. It has often been compared with the Shire from the Lord of the Rings, and understandably so. In Saksun, you can visit the local church, and near the church, there are many traditional old houses. But, if you decide to go to this part of the village, please respect the residents' privacy, since these are private homes, and do not look in through the windows.

If you are up for a walk, the trip to Saksun Beach is a short but scenic 20-minute hike.

You can drive to Saksun, where you can easily find the walking trails, the old village, and the church.

Kallur Lighthouse. Photo by Georgi Kalaydzhiev on Unsplash.

Kallur Lighthouse

Not only is this one of the most beautiful places in the Faroe Islands, but it is also relatively inaccessible. Firstly, the Kallur Lighthouse is out on the island Kalsoy, which isn't connected to the main islands, and secondly, it is a steep and long walk from the village Trøllanes. At any measure, this must be considered a hard climb.

It is here that the scenes from the James Bond movie No Time to Die were shot, including the infamous scene where Agent 007 dies. In his remembrance, the farmer who owns this land has raised a mock tombstone, which you can read about in the section about Cinematography in this book.

Tjørnuvík from above. Photo by Rúni í Múla.

Tjørnuvík Beach and Village

One of the most visited places on Streymoy is the northernmost village, Tjørnuvík. It is a small, cosy old village with many wooden houses and grass roofs. The village itself is surrounded by tall and impressive mountains, with a large sandy beach, from where you can see the Giant and the Hag.

If you decide to go to Tjørnuvík, know that the road is very narrow and that it follows a steep mountainside which is known for many landslides. The risk of landslides is highest when the rain is pouring, especially if it's after a dry season.

If you feel adventurous and you feel comfortable in the cold, wavy water, then you should consider looking up Faroe Islands Surf Guide, which is a local surfing company where you can rent surfing gear and boards. If you haven't tried surfing before, surfing lessons are also available.

See more at www.FaroeIslandsSurfGuide.com or get in touch by calling (+298) 25 88 98.

You can also try going to the Surf Shack, located by the beach, and see if you can book a lesson in person.

Chapter Twenty-Three

Hidden Gems in Nature

Many sites in the Faroes are free from tourists, and very few locals visit them. These gems are usually not commercialised by tourist agencies but are free to visit. If you decide to go, please respect the owners of the land.

Finding some of these places can be challenging, but with the help of your mobile phone and the Internet, you'll be able to find them easily. However, many places are not visible on apps such as Google Maps. Therefore, you must pay attention to the village names, which you can search for using your device.

Coordinates have been included in this second edition of the book, which you can use to find the exact location for each spot.

Salgjógv Beach. Photo by Rúni í Múla.

The Hidden Beach near Bøur

When you're driving between the villages Bø and Gásadalur in Vágar, there is a sandy beach hidden down by the shore in a gorge called Salgjógv. The high rock walls create shelter from the wind, and therefore, during the summer, it gets boiling on this beach.

How to get there:

The beach is between Bø and the tunnel opening leading to Gásadalur. It can be hard to find, but if you aim for a large skerry visible from the road above (the skerry is so prominent that you won't miss it) and head down towards it, you'll find the hidden beach by heading towards Bø.

Locals frequently go to the beach by boat, but you can also get there by foot. But this is only when the tide is low because when the tide is high, the way of entry is flooded.

You cannot go without asking permission first, which you can do by contacting Visit Vágar.

- **Coordinates**: ◻62°05'24.7"N, 7°23'56.1"W

Vatndalsvatn. Photo by Rúni í Múla.

Vatndalsvatn: The Heart-shaped Lake

One of the most "Instagram-worthy" places is the heart-shaped lake, Vatndalsvatn. The lake is situated in the mountains above Bø, in a valley between two mountain tops. There, by the lake, you are in raw nature, with no trace of civilisation except for a small mountain cottage. No sounds from driving cars, no light pollution in the evening, and no village are visible from the site.

How to get there:

When you drive from Sørvágur towards Bø, a large river, Breiðá, passes halfway between the two villages. If you follow the river Breiðá all the way up, you will reach the heart-shaped lake high in the mountains.

It is a steep climb to get there, and it is estimated to take an hour. However, it is considered a safe hike.

An alternative route is hiking uphill along the river that flows through the northern part of Sørvágur. When you reach the top of the hill, you might turn left and hike until you reach the heart-shaped lake.

- **Coordinates**: ☐62°05'31.2"N, 7°20'27.6"W

The Guardian of Fuglafjørður. Photo by Rúni í Múla.

The Guardian on Blue Mountain

Blábjørg, or Blue Mountain, is named for its blue tones when the weather is warm during the summer. The mountain is far away enough from Fuglafjørður that the warm summer air is seen colouring the dramatic mountain high above Fuglafjørður.

Blábjørg has a gorge called Mansgjógv, or the Man's Gorge. It gets its name from the stone pillar that stands in it, which, from the village, resembles a man. Some call him the guardian of Fuglafjørður.

How to get there:

A climb up to Blue Mountain and the Man in the Gorge is a moderately strenuous hike from Fuglafjørður. You can start your hike by walking up the valley west of the village, known as *Vesturi í Dal*. Start your hike from the waterfall and follow the river up the valley, where you'll see the Blue Mountain in front of you to your right. Continue through the valley all the way up to the mountain pass to the left of Blue Mountain. When you've reached that point, turn right, continuing behind the mountain ridge. Be careful not to climb the mountain top, as it will have you walking above the gorge where the Man is located.

Climbing the top is also an option, but if you wish, you should head directly up to it when you reach the mountain pass above the valley.

- **Coordinates**: ☐62°14'20.4"N, 6°51'50.4"W

Stone Stairs Above Gøta. Photo by Rúni í Múla.

The Mountain Trail Between Gøta and Leirvík

The old hiking road between Norðragøta and Leirvík has been used for centuries. It is one of the old public village routes, and hikers can use it without charge.

What makes this hike unique are the old stone stairs leading through the steep mountain, supported by steel railings, which are rare to come by on any Faroese hiking route. Unlike other places, several stairs are built in the steep landscape, which is fascinating to look at and admire, accompanied by the magnificent view over the fjords and mountains.

Although this hiking route is popular with locals and is not in any way hidden, it isn't that well-known either, although it is free for the public to roam.

How to get there:

There is a football field in the valley above Leirvík, which you can find by heading up the road that leads through the forested area high in the village. There, by the football clubhouse, you can find a sign that shows you the directions for the village route, which is marked by cairns and small wooden pillars painted in a clearly visible colour.

You can also hike the other way around, although this makes for a much more strenuous hike. But if you wish to do so, you can find the start of the village path by heading for the old centre of Norðragøta, with tiny black houses with grass roofs by the old church. There, you will find a sign showing you the way, and you will be led up the old trail by following the same wooden pillars and old cairns.

- **Coordinates Leirvík:** 62°12'16.0"N 6°42'55.0"W

- **Coordinates Norðragøta:** 62°11'52.3"N 6°44'21.5"W

Kluftá River. Photo by Rúni í Múla.

The Hidden River of Kluftá

One of the most iconic areas in the Faroese nature is the river Kluftá. This river hides many enjoyable natural areas, even though it is close to the village and cannot be seen down from the village.

If you decide to go, please do not swim in the river since it is the drinking water of Vík, the village below.

How to get there:

When you're in the village Vík, park your car and head towards the large stream that flows through the village centre, bypassing the octagonal church.

Follow the river up the mountainside by entering one of the gates in the fences blocking the trail up. By doing this, you'll get there.

- **Coordinates**: □62°16'36.3"N, 7°06'27.4"W

Stakkurin

In the summer, and during sheep herding, people go out in the sea stack, known as Stakkurin, using a telpher line. High above the sea, people sit in a small open carriage that gets pulled to and from the stack.

One can only get onto the sea stack by hiring a local guide with access to the telpher system. The carriage is locked so that it cannot be used without a key to unlock it.

If you are afraid of heights, this trip is not recommended, and if you aren't usually afraid of heights, this trip might well be too challenging for you. But, if you are brave enough, it is a fantastic experience that you cannot try in other places around the Faroe Islands.

If you wish to go, you can contact the tour guide at stakkurtours@hotmail.com or (+298) **26 63 43**. The trips to the sea stacks are not part of any commercialised tours, and you might have to ask very politely to be able to go.

- **Coordinates**: ☐62°18'33.2"N, 7°10'18.5"W

Deserted Terrain in Kirkjubøreyn. Photo by Rúni í Múla.

Kirkjubøreyn: The Dessert Moon Landscape

In the old village path between Kirkjubø and Tórshavn, there is a large desert area on the top of the mountains. You are entirely away from civilisation in a vast rocky area, in a terrain unlike anywhere else on the Faroe Islands.

This place is not part of any tourist attraction, and very few locals ever walk this area.

If you decide to go, **you must notify someone before going**, and **bring a fully charged mobile phone**, as you cannot expect to meet anyone in that part of the mountains.

How to get there:

You can get to this area by walking up the mountainside in Kirkjubø, starting by the cattle grid when you enter the village. From there, you head up the mountain, following a narrow path leading towards Tórshavn. When you see the path dividing into two, take the one leading you to the top of the hill.

- **Coordinates**: ☐62°05'24.7"N, 7°23'56.1"W

Water Dam in Vestmanna. Photo by Rúni í Múla.

The Water Dams in Vestmanna

Above the village of Vestmanna, a network of water dams and tunnels provides a large part of the electricity on the Faroe Islands. The dams are some of the oldest still in-use electricity plants on the islands and are relatively large.

How to get there:

It can be tricky to find the way up since the roads in Vestmanna can be pretty confusing. But, when you arrive at the village, you turn to your first right and then your first right again, and you'll reach the dams. The roads are narrow and in poor shape, but they are driveable.

Be careful and respect the signs that have been put up. They have been placed there for a very good reason, and not respecting them can be dangerous!

- **Coordinates:** 61°49'35.2"N, 6°48'39.8"W

The Splashing Hole. Photo by Rúni í Múla.

Spruttholið – The Splashing Hole

Spruttholið is a natural cleft and cave into the bedrock near the village of Sandur, Sandoy. Seen from land, the cleft has two openings connected by a sea cave that leads out to the sea. Because of the always strong current in Faroese waters, the sea always splashes, but when the current is strong, the splashes become very dramatic and can be seen reaching high into the sky.

How to get there:

Sandur village, Sandoy, has a small boat harbour south of the village. It is where you catch the ferry to Skúvoy. If you face the harbour and your back faces the village, Spruttholið can be found on the headland to your right.

- **Coordinates:** 61°49'35.2"N, 6°48'39.8"W

The Sandy Hills of Mølheyggjar

Mølheyggjar is a protected beach in Sandur, Sandoy. The sandy hills have formed due to plants that grow there, whose roots hold the sand dunes together. Mølheyggjar is unique to the Faroe Islands, as this is the only place where such dunes can be found.

Although Mølheyggjar cannot be said to be a hidden treasure, it is an underestimated place to visit.

How to get there:

In Sandur, between the two village districts, you see the sandy hills by the shore. You cannot miss them.

- **Coordinates**: 61°29'29.4"N, 6°51'46.9"W

Akraberg Cliffs and Lighthouse. Photo by Bo Peng on Unsplash.

The Light House on Akraberg and the Frisian Colony

South of the village of Sumba, you find Akraberg, where there are a few houses and a lighthouse. It is said that a Frisian colony once lived here, which for hundreds of years lived parallel to the Norse settlers of the Faroe Islands.

In Akraberg, you'll find a phenomenal view, which the lighthouse only enhances. It is a picturesque scene, perfect for your social media accounts.

Akraberg is easy to drive to, but the road is poor, though driveable.

How to get there:

In the village of Sumba, you can see a small, narrow road leading into the mountains. It is recommended that you drive on that road, whether you intend to go to Akraberg or take a scenic route, as it is one of the Buttercup routes (see p. 223).

When you drive up this road, you'll find a crossroad, where the narrow road also continues to your right. Follow that road all the way out, and you'll get there.

It can be challenging to find this road, so don't hesitate to ask the locals for directions.

- **Coordinates**: 61°23'42.0"N, 6°40'56.5"W

The Wooden Bridge to Rituskorð. Photo by Rúni í Múla.

Cleft Rituskorð

In the mountains above Sandvík in Suðuroy, to the west of the village, there is a wooden bridge, high above a deep gorge, that leads all the way down into the sea. If you are afraid of heights, this trip is not recommended. If you, however, are in for a thrilling experience, walking this bridge can do it for you.

It is moderately easy to hike from the village, as you can follow an old road most of the way. The entire trip is an estimated 40-minute hike.

Disclaimer: Walking on the bridge is at its own risk, and only one person is allowed at a time!

If you decide to go, be careful of your surroundings and not go too close to the edge.

How to get there:

In Sandvík, you'll see a small road or trail that leads up through the valley, surpassing the river of Sandvíksá. Follow that road all the way up until you see the cliff edges. You can find the bridge on your left-hand side facing the cliff edge when you approach the end of the road.

- **Coordinates**: 61°37'49.6"N, 6°58'56.8"W

The Holið í Helli Cave. Photo by Rúni í Múla.

Holið í Helli: The Troll Cave

In Froðba, there is a cave where it is said that a troll woman resides. This cave is by the shore, and when the tide is high, the cave isn't accessible. When the tide is low, you can walk in. The cave is filled with water-rolled stones, which form a rocky beach within it.

How to get there:

When you're in Froðba, Suðuroy, drive as far to the east as possible. There you'll find a small parking space and a bench. There, you'll also find a fence with a gate. Walk through it and head north, straight ahead through the gate. There, you'll find it.

- **Coordinates:** 61°32'53.9"N, 6°44'46.6"W

Botnur Road. Photo by Rúni í Múla.

The Most Rural Places Accessible by Car

In the mountains above Vágur, Suðuroy, a narrow road leads beyond the mountains. Following this road, you can visit three distinct places, all among the top three most rural places you can visit by car.

One of these places is the small village of Fámará, which accounts for only one farm that has been abandoned for years. The road leading there is rough, and driving there without an SUV **is not advisable**.

The two other places are the village of Botnur, which only accounts for one house and two other power plant buildings, and Lake Ryskivatn, which lies above Botnur, where the power plant gets water from the water turbines. You can drive to Botnur and Lake Ryskivatn, but the road and the steep mountainsides are rough. Therefore, it is not recommended that anyone who isn't an experienced driver go there by car. It isn't recommended for anyone afraid of heights, either.

If you wish to visit these places without driving, you can hike there by following a path made for that purpose.

How to get there:

Both Botnur and Ryskivatn are accessible by Google Maps; Fámará is not. But if you tap in Botnur or Ryskivatn on Google Maps, you will get to the narrow road leading to all three places. On the road, road signs lead you to all three places, with Fármará road leading in a different direction, which you can see by a crossroad.

If you wish to hike, you can find the route by either following the road or the walking trails, which you can find on the information signs in the village of Vágur. The information signs are located in the village centre.

- **Coordinates Fámará**: 61°32'53.9"N, 6°44'46.6"W

- **Coordinates Botnur**: 61°29'09.9"N, 6°52'10.8"W

- **Coordinates Ryskivatn**: 61°29'29.4"N, 6°51'46.9"W

Chapter Twenty-Four

How to Get Around

It can be tricky to get around in the Faroe Islands. Depending on your needs, you should consider whether you'd like to rely on public transportation or you should rent a car. Public transport can take you to most places, though it can be tricky to visit some rural areas. If you wish to see the larger towns, public transportation is a very well-suited way.

If you rent a car, most larger islands have car ferries, which you can take but cannot book in advance. If you choose to bring your vehicle onto a ferry, you should be by the ferry in good time (at least an hour before the scheduled time).

Public Transportation

Strandferðarskip Landsins is a public transportation company. On their website, schedules for ferries and buses can be found. Cancellations are notified on their website if stormy or misty weather affects any offered routes.

See more: www.ssl.fo/en/

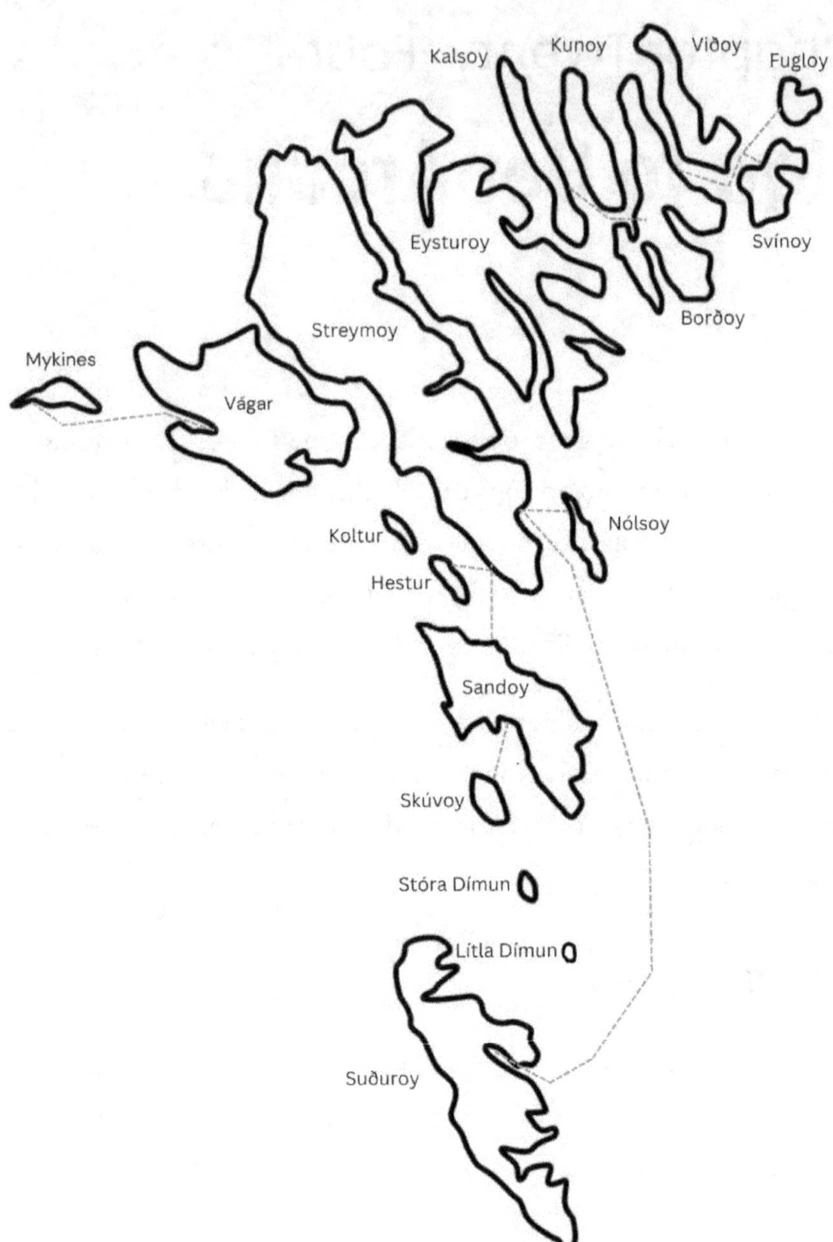

Sailing Routes Between the Islands. Graphics by Rúni í Múla.

Helicopter Landing. Photo by KarelZe on Pixabay.

Helicopters

The Faroese airline, Atlantic Airways, offers transportation by helicopter to some islands. When the helicopter is en route, you can travel by air for a decent prize, with prizes varying from 255 DKK to 1080 DKK. However, if you wish to travel by helicopter, booking must be made ahead.

The helicopter can also be rented for 35.000 DKK per hour, and there are some high-end tours, including sightseeing on the island of Vágar and a James Bond tour flown on the island of Kallsoy.

See more: www.atlanticairways.fo/en

Helicopter Routes Between Islands and Towns. Graphics by Rúni í Múla.

Rental cars

Driving your car is the easiest way to get around in the Faroes. It isn't always easy to get around using public transportation, especially if you want to visit some of the rural places. Also, driving allows you to choose more scenic routes, which can only add to your travelling experience. Car rental can be expensive, though.

There are many car rental options. A complete list is available on the website for Vagar Airport.

See more: www.fae.fo

Toll Roads

All subsea tunnels are toll roads. Therefore, it is advised to check the prices before driving through them.

Prices:

Norðuroyartunnilin, the subsea tunnel between Eysturoy and Borðoy:

<u>100 DKK</u>
<u>20 DKK</u> with a tunnel subscription.

Vágatunnilin, the subsea tunnel between Streymoy and Vágar:

<u>100 DKK</u>
<u>20 DKK</u> with a tunnel subscription.

Eysturoyartunnilin, the subsea tunnel between Eysturoy and Streymoy:

<u>175 DKK</u>
<u>75 DKK</u> with a tunnel subscription.

See more: www.tunnil.fo

If you decide to rent a car, **always ask if the rental includes a tunnel subscription**, as some renters charge high additional fees. Tolls can be paid at the nearby tank stations.

The Buttercup Roads

These roads are marked with a buttercup sign, and generally, these roads are more scenic and have lesser traffic than others. But, some of these roads are in rough shape, which is worth considering before you go.

List of Buttercup Routes:

- The Road to Gásadalur (Vágar).

- The Road to Saksun (Streymoy).

- The Road to Múla (Borðoy).

- The Road to Oyndarfjørður (Eysturoy).

- The Road to Elduvík (Eysturoy).

- The Road between Eiði, Funningsfjørður and Gjógv (Eysturoy).

- The Road to Tjørnuvík (Streymoy).

- The Road between Nes, Æðuvík and Runavík (Eysturoy).

- The Mountain Road between Tórshavn and Kollafjørður (Streymoy).

- The Mountain Road between Lopra, Víkarbyrgi and Sumba (Suðuroy).

- The Mountain Road from Øravík to Hov (Suðuroy).

Another unofficial road is the Mountain Road between Leirvík and Fuglafjørður (Eysturoy).

Chapter Twenty-Five

Contact Information and Safety Measures

If you decide to travel to the Faroe Islands, here is some crucial information you must consider before going. These safety measures are highly inspired by the formal safety guidelines proposed by the Faroese authorities. Alternative to the advice brought forth here, it is advised to seek out Visit Faroe Islands's brochure, *Guide to Safe Hiking*.

Clothing

The weather in the Faroe Islands is almost always wet and cold. Even in the summer, when the weather can be good, it is not guaranteed to stay that way. Therefore, it is essential that you bring warm and waterproof clothing if you plan to go – especially if part of your trip is planned out in nature.

If you're hiking, don't wear slippery clothes, as it can be very dangerous to slip on the steep mountainsides. Also, remember always to wear proper hiking shoes.

Hiking

It is legal to hike in most places in the mountains. However, there are some restricted areas and some seasons that make the trips either illegal or not advisable. If you plan to hike, always remember to ask or notify the local tourist information office. The phone number of the local tourist information office is in the chapter *Important Phone Numbers*.

If you decide to go on a hike, then please follow the following instructions:

- Never hike alone. When or if possible, you should hire a local guide.

- Never hike in foggy weather.

- Never hike in pouring rain or during a storm.

- Always check the weather forecast before leaving. The weather can change quicker than you can imagine.

- Keep away from cliff edges.

- Respect fences and signs that are put up for tourists and hikers.

- Investigate seasonal farming and hunting activities.

- Never wear slippery clothes or shoes when hiking.

- Remember to wear warm and waterproof clothing.

- Hiking boots are recommended.

- If you plan on taking a long hike, remember to eat before you go, and preferably bring something edible and drinkable with you.

- Litter is disposed of in trash bins. Bring the litter with you until you return home if you can't find one.

- Always inform someone before you go on a hike. If you don't know anyone, contact the local tourist information centre.

- Remember to bring a fully charged phone with you.

- Do not hike during the hare hunting season, which is from 2nd November to 31st December.

- Sheep herding activities are in the spring and fall. If you see people herding sheep, keep away.

Safety Measures for Driving

If you decide to rent a car, here is some need-to-know information crucial for safe driving. Many more scenic roads are narrow, so you must be extra careful while driving.

- Be careful of sheep roaming the main roads, especially on the smaller, more narrow scenic roads.

- If you drive on narrow roads, remember to use the lay-by for oncoming traffic.

- If you are driving downhill, then make sure to stop for the oncoming traffic that is driving uphill.

- Some tunnels have only one lane. Be careful when driving in those tunnels, and remember to respect the oncoming traffic by using the lay-by.

- The speed limit is 80 kilometres per hour, so please do not drive any faster or slower than 80 kilometres per hour.

- Off-road driving is prohibited by law.

- Do not drink and drive.

- Remember to turn on the headlights.

- Remember to fasten your seatbelts.

- Talking on a handheld telephone is prohibited by law.

- Drive safely.

Important websites

Visit Faroe Islands: www.visitfaroeislands.fo

Guide to Faroe Islands: www.guidetofaroeislands.fo

Public Transportation: www.ssl.fo

Atlantic Airways: www.ssl.fo

Take-away: www.menu.fo

Online phone book: www.sona.fo

The Official Site of the Faroe Islands: www.faroeislands.fo

Important Phone Numbers

Emergency calls

Emergency Calls: 112

Police Station: 114

Doctor:118

Taxi Companies

Taxi Bil: (+298) 32 32 32

Mini Buss Taxa: (+298) 21 21 21

Taxa Snar: (+298) 77 77 78

Auto: (+298) 36 36 36

Hotels

Hotel Føroyar: (+298) 31 75 00

Hotel Hafnia: (+298) 31 32 33

Hotel Tórshavn: (+298) 35 00 00

Hotel Brandan: (+298) 30 92 00

Hilton Garden Inn: (+298) 41 40 00

Hotel Djurhuus: (+298) 35 55 00

Havgrím Seaside Hotel: (+298) 20 14 00

62N Hotel: (+298) 50 06 00

Hotel Runavík: (+298) 66 33 33

Hotel Klaksvík: (+298) 45 53 33

Hotel Norð: (+298) 45 12 44

Hotel Tvøroyri: (+298)□37 11 71

Hotel Bakkin: (+298) 25 04 44

Gamla Hotellið Magenta: (+298) 28 64 08

Giljanes Hostel: (+298) 33 34 65

Camping

Vágur Camping: (+298) 23 93 90

Trongisvágur Camping: (+298) 61 10 80

Fámjin Camping: (+298) 37 20 46

Hvalba Camping: (+298) 23 75 65

Dalur Camping: (+298) 21 79 01

Sandur Camping: (+298) 22 20 78

Giljanes Camping: (+298) 33 34 65

Mykines Camping: (+298) 21 29 85

Tórshavn Camping: (+298) 30 24 25

Vestmanna Camping: (+298) 21 22 45

Lómundaroyri Camping: (+298) 42 40 01

Víkar Camping: (+298) 28 61 99

Eiði Camping: (+298) 21 93 77

Fuglafjørður Camping: (+298) 23 80 15

Elduvík Camping: (+298) 41 70 60

Gjógv Camping: (+298) 42 31 71

Æðuvík Camping: (+298) 22 17 68

Svínoy Camping: (+298) 45 69 39

Mikladalur Camping: (+298) 45 69 39

Tourist Information Centres

Visit Faroe Islands: (+298) 66 65 55

Visit Suðuroy: (+298) 61 10 80 and (+298) 23 93 90

Visit Sandoy: (+298) 22 20 78 and (+298) 72 01 00

Visit Vágar: (+298) 33 34 55

Visit Tórshavn: (+298) 30 24 25

Visit Nólsoy: (+298) 52 70 60

Visit Eysturoy: (+298) 23 80 15 and (+298) 41 70 60

Visit Norðoy: (+298) 45 69 39

Also by Rúni í Múla

The Obscure and Fun Facts of the Faroe Islands: *A Travel Guide and Alternative Introduction to Faroese Society and Culture*

Hiking in the Faroe Islands: *A Complete Hiker's Guide to All Public Walking Trails and Routes*